Owen Wister

Twayne's United States Authors Series

David J. Nordloh, Editor
Indiana University, Bloomington

TUSAS 475

OWEN WISTER

at the Mammoth Hot Springs, 1887

Photograph courtesy of Frances K. W. Stokes

Owen Wister

By John L. Cobbs
Ursinus College

Twayne Publishers • Boston

Owen Wister

John L. Cobbs

Copyright © 1984 by G. K. Hall & Company
All Rights Reserved
Published by Twayne Publishers
A Division of G. K. Hall & Company
70 Lincoln Street
Boston, Massachusetts 02111

Book Production by Elizabeth Todesco

Book Design by Barbara Anderson

Printed on permanent/durable acid-free
paper and bound in the United States of
America.

**Library of Congress Cataloging in
Publication Data.**

Cobbs, John L.
   Owen Wister.

   (Twayne's United States authors series ; TUSAS 475)
   Bibliography: p. 127
   Includes index.
   1. Wister, Owen, 1860–1938—
Criticism and interpretation.
I. Title.   II. Series.
PS3346.C6   1984   813'.52   84-4688
ISBN 0-8057-7416-5

In memory of C. Hugh Holman,
who started me down this trail
and taught me to ride

Contents

About the Author

John L. Cobbs teaches English at Ursinus College. He received a B.A. from Haverford College and a Ph.D. in English from the University of North Carolina at Chapel Hill where he taught film criticism and composition for five years.

Professor Cobbs has published a number of articles on American literature, including recent studies of black poetry *(CLA Journal)*, William Styron *(Mississippi Quarterly)*, Peter Matthiessen *(Dictionary of Literary Biography)*, Albert Pike *(Southern Literature)*, and Hemingway *(South Atlantic Bulletin)*, and several contributions to the *John O'Hara Journal*. He is currently working on a book-length study of Hemingway's female characters and a novel set in coastal South Carolina.

Preface

It is eighty years since the publication of Owen Wister's *The Virginian,* and the novel finally seems to be fading from the public eye. Only recently have literary historians as well as the reading public forgotten the enormous impact of that book on the American imagination. At its publication in 1902, it was the most popular book in the country, and for three generations it remained the most respected, widely read, and influential American Western. It literally invented and established the figure of the Western hero—a figure so endlessly copied, reworked, and reissued that critical discussion of this colossus of popular culture cannot ignore its mythological stature.

Even as the Virginian retreats to his eventual niche in literary histories—perhaps under the rubric "Regional Characters: Prototypes"— his descendants flourish. From the novels of Louis L'Amour to the films of John Wayne, the Virginian has endured as the archetype for hundreds of cowboy heroes. Interestingly, his persistence is strongest in popular "art" outside of literature—film, television, comics, and a plethora of commercial incarnations from dolls to capguns.

For the modern world, the Virginian in various popular and artistic forms is Wister's only legacy. Although the novel remained popular through the thirty-five years its author lived after writing it, his literary career declined steadily after the turn of the century. Hardly exceptional even during his publishing prime in the 1890s, Wister's fictional output thinned after *The Virginian* and almost ceased after the death of his wife in 1913. By the time he died in 1937, all his writing except that novel had been long out of print, and few readers could name anything else he had written. A revival of interest in early Western fiction after midcentury brough reissues of other Western writers—Zane Gray and Eugene Manlove Rhodes in particular— but Wister's audience continued to shrink. No Wister renaissance is in sight today.

The neglect of Wister is unfortunate not only because he was a substantial influence as the creator of the popular cowboy, but also because he was a fine writer who produced a significant body of distinguished fiction. His Western canon alone should win him a stature equal to that of less accomplished writers of regional literature like Bret Harte, George Washington Cable, and Joel Chandler Harris. Ironically, despite its endurance, *The Virginian* is arguably neither Wister's finest work of art nor his most accurate picture of life on the Western frontier. Many of the tales he gathered into four story collections show greater craftsmanship and a more honest and realistic treatment of the rich variety of Western life. Yet they are virtually unread.

The Western writings must stand as Wister's major claim to literary distinction, but even without them he would have significance as a historical figure and a man of letters. A Harvard-educated Philadelphia aristocrat, Wister held an important position in America's ruling class. In an era when nearly all major American writers lacked formal education and came from the lower middle class, only Edith Wharton held a comparable position. Wister was a close friend of Theodore Roosevelt, Henry Cabot Lodge, and Oliver Wendell Holmes, Jr., a force in Philadelphia reform politics, and an acknowledged intellectual and cultural leader of the Eastern establishment. For better or worse, his opinions made an impact, and for half a century his voice was heard—denouncing machine politics, decrying immigration, calling for American intervention in World War I, proposing Sinclair Lewis for membership in the American Academy of Arts and Letters. He spent a lifetime expressing his opinions, as men of his class did, not as an exercise in egotism, but as a responsibility. In speeches, public and private letters, articles, and books, he worked to shape a world in which he saw himself, justifiably, as a major actor. His writings on public affairs are even less read today than his fiction, but they are worth study as the record of the life of a man who was a significant voice in his times.

If only as the first, the most popular, and the most articulate and artistic interpreter of the frontier West in fiction, Wister deserves careful critical attention. He was the author of a body of work that still stands as the clearest literary statement of a theme that has obsessed the imagination of America and the world. He defined the frontier West at the very moment that it was yielding its particularity to the forces of the amorphous future. In doing so, he captured a regional experience singularly critical to the formation of the American character. Wister's cowboy world did much to forge in the national mind the eventual consciousness of the genre.

As an influence Wister should be studied; as an artist he should be read. Despite occasional structural awkwardness and spots of florid rhetoric, he is in the main a fine craftsman and a rewarding story-teller. An hour or two spent with *The Virginian* or many of the short stories can be far more satisfying than a tendentious dose of most of Wister's better known contemporaries. Wister's place in literary history is secure, but it is regrettable that he so seldom is read by Americans whose image he did much to create and who might find him good company.

John L. Cobbs

Ursinus College

Chronology

1860 Owen Wister born in Philadelphia, Pennsylvania, 14 July.

1870 Goes to Europe for three years; attends boarding school first in Switzerland, then in England.

1873 Enrolls in exclusive St. Paul's School, Concord, New Hampshire.

1878 Enrolls at Harvard, where he is a member of Hasty Pudding, Porcellian, Dickey. Meets Theodore Roosevelt, John Jay Chapman, and other influential friends.

1882 Graduates summa cum laude. Publishes *The New Swiss Family Robinson*, reprint of *Harvard Lampoon* series. Goes to Europe to study music, plays for Franz Liszt.

1883 Recalled by father to Philadelphia for business career.

1885 Writes Realist novel, *A Wise Man's Son*, but does not publish it, at advice of friend William Dean Howells. On verge of a nervous breakdown, visits Wyoming for several months for his health—the first of fifteen extended trips in the next few years. Begins journal. Enters Harvard Law School.

1891 Resolves to become a writer of Western fiction. Writes first stories.

1892 Begins publishing stories in *Harper's Monthly*.

1893 Meets Frederic Remington in Wyoming.

1895 "The Evolution of the Cowboy," essay delineating Wister's vision of cowboy character. *Red Men and White*, his first book of Western stories.

1897 *Lin McLean*, Western novel.

1898 Marries Mary Channing Wister, his cousin.

1900 *The Jimmyjohn Boss*, Western story collection.

1901 *Ulysses S. Grant*, short biography; *Philosophy 4*, very short novel.

1902 *The Virginian*, Western novel, becomes immediate best-seller.

1903   Fails to adapt *The Virginian* for the stage; tours with the road company of eventual dramatization.

1906   *Lady Baltimore,* novel of manners about Charleston, South Carolina.

1907   *The Seven Ages of Washington,* biography.

1909   Mysterious illness leaves Wister bedridden for more than a year.

1910   Returns to Wyoming to regain his health.

1911   *Members of the Family,* Western story collection.

1912   Active in politics; runs for Philadelphia City Council, loses; begins novel about Philadelphia.

1913   Death of Mary Channing Wister in August.

1914   Travels in Europe just before outbreak of World War I.

1916   *The Pentecost of Calamity,* book-length essay favoring American intervention in war and attacking Germany.

1921   *A Straight Deal or the Ancient Grudge,* book-length political essay.

1922   *Neighbors Henceforth,* completes political trilogy.

1923   *Watch Your Thirst,* comic antitemperance drama.

1924   Begins working on Western stories after thirteen-year hiatus.

1928   *When West Was West,* Western story collection.

1930   *Roosevelt: The Story of a Friendship.*

1938   Dies in North Kingston, Rhode Island, 14 July. Buried in Philadelphia.

Chapter One

The Trail to Success

Feudal Philadelphia

That the man who created the prototype for the most enduring of American folk heroes, the cowboy, should have been a pedigreed aristocrat, a Harvard-educated Philadelphia lawyer, and a patrician by moral conviction is an irony of such vulgarity that Owen Wister himself would have scorned it. But it is true; the forces that directed Wister's life were those of birth, breeding, and carefully cultivated gentility. The legacy of his writing was the establishment of a character whose mythic image is imbedded in the consciousness of the American *lumpenproletariat*. Like the ball park hotdog, the cowboy belongs to the people, and Wister gave him to them.

He was born 14 July 1860 at the family estate in Germantown, now part of Philadelphia. The Wisters were not truly, as Alexander Woollcott later accused, "deep-dyed feudal Philadelphia aristocracy,"[1] but they were so much the cream of the upper middle class that Owen Wister can lay claim to being the best born and bred of all modern American writers. Consciousness of social class and a sense of social responsibility were major forces shaping his writing and life.

Sarah Butler Wister, his mother, was the child of one of the most celebrated marriages of the nineteenth century. Her mother, Fanny Kemble, was the most popular Shakespearean actress of the day, a member of the great English acting dynasty. Fanny's husband, Owen's grandfather, was the grandson of a South Carolinian signer of the Constitution and heir to a rice plantation in the Sea Islands. Fanny Kemble was a great beauty, but hardly typical of retiring early Victorian womanhood. She published six volumes of poetry and *Journal of a Residence on a Georgian Plantation in 1838–1839,* a famous account of her brief life as mistress of Pierce Butler's little rice kingdom.[2] Published in 1863, largely to defend Yankee abolitionism to the pro-Confederate English during the Civil War, the book was widely read on both sides of the Atlantic and was credited with swaying English public opinion against British intervention on the side of the South.

Fanny's marriage had long since disintegrated—in 1847—for, in addition to her strong abolitionist feelings, she had found life as a southern belle and a Philadelphia grande dame too confining. After a messy divorce,[3] she went back on the stage, but kept Butler Place just outside Philadelphia, where Owen Wister spent much of his childhood and over which she presided periodically in dramatic splendor, turning it into a Philadelphia replica of a southern manor house.

In Fanny Kemble's absence, and after her death in 1893, Butler Place was ruled by her daughter, Sarah Butler Wister, Owen's mother. She was an acidulous woman—beautiful and charming, but cold, haughty, and militantly intellectual, with an obsession about the cultivation of art and the maintenance of "standards." Sarah Butler Wister spoke French and Italian fluently, played several musical instruments, and read voraciously—all habits she passed on to her son. She wrote unsigned essays for the *Atlantic Monthly,* several expressing concern about "the low state of American political affairs" in the 1870s.[4] She had, if we are to believe Fanny Kemble's memoirs, "a remarkable incapacity to maintain tolerable relations with individuals 'beneath her station,' "[5] and she was notorious for her problems with servants.[6] Henry James, a close friend, wrote of her, "She is intensely conscious and diffident and lacks a certain repose comfortable to herself and others."[7]

Her influence on her only child, Owen, was profound. For more than thirty-five years, from the time he was ten and left home until his mother's death in 1908, he wrote his mother at length every week and received longer letters in return—letters full of reproach, advice, and direction, constantly passing judgment upon her son and upon the world. Years after Wister's death, his daughter wrote, "Perhaps it was his mother's impossibly high standard in all intellectual matters and her cerebral approach to life that made him diffident. Apparently she had never allowed him to feel that he came up to her expectation."[8]

It may not have been a warm mother-son relationship, but it was a binding one. Sarah Butler Wister's overbearing projection of an aristocratic mien and self-conscious fostering of the arts dominated the direction of her son's life. Wister always credited his artistic nature to his mother's side of the family,[9] and doubtless the arrogant concern with race and breeding that informs Wister's fiction was also her legacy. His mother made him "a strange, withdrawn, talented boy,"[10] and through his long life, there was always to be a formality in his bearing and a reserve in dealing with people.

Under his mother's direction, Wister spent a strictly regimented childhood. He showed an early talent for music, which she encouraged forcefully. He soon spoke French as fluently as English, and his precocious reading assured his success as a student. The family traveled a great deal, and Wister often visited his Butler relatives in the South, but it was apparently a rather precious life. In a pathetic letter to his mother just before he went to college, Wister wrote: "I have never camped out and gone shooting and lots of boys have and I feel a big desire to do so too. . . . I don't want to be a 'house boy' and have tried not to."[11] It would be eight more years after this letter before Wister would first see Wyoming, but he was already predisposed to find in its wild, free, masculine life the antidote to the rigidity of his cramped childhood.

Despite the strength of his wife's character and her overpowering influence on her son, Dr. Owen Jones Wister, Owen's father, was not a weak or inconsequential man. He was, though, a strangely shadowy one, at least in the family letters and chronicles which give so vivid a picture of his wife. He came from a line of prosperous Philadelphia merchants who had originally emigrated to America in 1727 after a Continental tradition of service as foresters to the royalty of the German Palatinate. Although apparently conservative in politics and disposition, he was an active man, working hard as a country doctor, rather than treating his profession lightly as many gentleman dilettantes did. Dr. Wister shared his wife's love for travel, and he had sailed around the world in 1848 while serving in the navy.[12] He may have been "as relaxed as his wife was intense and as pedestrian as she was imaginative,"[13] but he cannot have been wholly dull, for he was known for his sense of humor, and Henry James, notably intolerant of poor conversation, evidently enjoyed his company as well as that of his intellectually aggressive wife.[14] Two other aspects of Dr. Wister's character emerge from the family records: he was a firm churchgoer and he disliked music, whether as a pastime or a career; the latter was to have sad consequences for his highly musical only son.

What we do not know of Dr. Wister is perhaps more significant. For all the extended correspondence Owen Wister had with his mother, he had little with his father, and he apparently almost never spoke or wrote of him either before or after the doctor's death.[15] The question of his son's career evidently weighed heavily on the doctor's mind, and his few letters to Owen, even when his son was a young boy, speak of the need for finding a profession that would be both profitable and responsible. The conflict over career was to deepen over the years, and Dr. Wister eventually forced Owen out of a promising future as a composer and into the unwelcome practice of first banking, then law. Owen's resentment of his father's heavy-handed direction may have come between the two men, but it paved the way for the younger man's escape West and into the writing of fiction.

From the time he was ten years old, Owen Wister spent little of his life at home with his parents. He first went to boarding schools in Switzerland for a year while they traveled on the Continent with Fanny Kemble, and then he lived for a year in England with his mother's sister. In 1873 he enrolled at St. Paul's School in Concord, New Hampshire, where he stayed until he went to Harvard five years later.

St. Paul's was, and still is, one of the best preparatory schools in America, both socially and academically. Strongly Episcopalian, although not strictly a "church school," it stressed firm grounding in the classics and a Spartan life, following the English model. Wister did well academically, and was evidently popular and happy. Predictably, he was active in music, the school's library association, and the literary magazine,[16] which he eventually edited and to which he contributed his first published story, "Down in a Diving Bell," "a light piece, foreshadowing the humor of his later writing."[17]

In 1878 Wister enrolled at Harvard, thus completing the natural progression of sons of the American ruling class: from socially prominent family, to distinguished preparatory school, to Ivy League college. His four years at Cambridge deeply affected the rest of his life. There he met his friends Theodore Roosevelt, Henry Cabot Lodge, and many other members of America's establishment. Wister got on well with the rich and powerful, and he enjoyed their company. At Harvard he was a member of the elite Porcelian and Hasty Pudding clubs, and the even more exclusive, semisecret, Rabelaisian Dickey, of which Wister wrote years later, "To be left out of the Dickey meant that your social future at Harvard was likely to be in the back seats,"[18] where Wister took a great pride in not sitting.

Unlike many other young gentlemen of good family and some of his friends, Wister was a spectacularly good student, and it was as a summa cum laude Phi Beta Kappa that he graduated in 1882. His academic record was in large part a function of his continued absorption with literature of all types, and of his growing commitment to music, increasingly as a potential profession rather than an avocation. He had decided before graduation to become a composer. His first major composition, the words and music for a light opera *Dido and Aeneas,* was produced by the Hasty Pudding Club his senior year. He was still writing, too, producing stories for the Harvard literary magazines. His first published book, a casual satiric fantasy called *The New Swiss Family Robinson* (1882) was a reprint of a series Wister ran in the *Lampoon* that year. It was an inconsequential piece of escapist fantasy and parody, but good enough to rate a letter of commendation from Mark Twain.

In the summer of 1882, Wister left for Europe for an indefinite time to study music. In August, through a letter of introduction from Fanny Kemble, he played one of his own compositions for Franz Liszt at Wagner's house in Beyreuth and was rewarded when the famous composer wrote to his grandmother approving Wister's talent and by implication his choice of a career.[19] Wister then went to Paris, studying music under Ernest Guiraud of the prestigious Conservatoire. He was sure he had found his calling. But then, in the middle of 1883, his father wired him to come home to find a respectable job.

Bitterly, Wister "went below stairs into the Union Safe Deposit Vaults . . . and sat on a high hard stool computing interest."[20] He would loathe bankers and banking for the rest of his life. He stuck it out for more than a year and then wrote his father begging to escape so he could go to Harvard Law School, although he was hardly more enthusiastic about the law than about business. Thus Wister found himself at twenty-four with his education complete, his hopes of a life as a composer crushed, failed in a business career, and desolately facing an alternative that offered as little chance of fulfillment. There was not much to indicate that he was about to find himself and in the strangest of places—Wyoming.

These two years after Wister's return to America were not entirely fruitless. He spent a lot of time at the newly organized Tavern Club, cementing old friendships and developing new ones. One of the few non-Harvard members of the club was its first president, William Dean Howells, who had recently finished his distinguished stint as editor of the *Atlantic Monthly* and was rapidly becoming the most influential voice in American literature. Howells was then working on *The Rise of Silas Lapham* and was at the height of his creative powers, producing a pure Realism in fiction that had yet to suffer the muddling effects of social propaganda. Certainly inspired by Howells, and perhaps directly at his instigation, Wister produced, with some help from his cousin Langdon Mitchell, a two-hundred-thousand-word novel.

He titled it *A Wise Man's Son* and asked Howells to read it. Howells did and immediately advised Wister never to show the manuscript to a publisher. *A Wise Man's Son* was the realistic story of a young American, born to be a painter but forced into a business career by an unsympathetic father and "the general American idea." Howells praised the work, but felt that "coming from a young American, it was certain to shock the public gravely; it was full of hard swearing, hard drinking, too much knowledge of good and evil." Worse, there was a character named the Widow Taylor whom, Howells said, "a whole fig tree would not cover."[21] Deferring to Howells's judgment and reputation, Wister shelved the book, and it is now apparently irretrievably lost.

Wister, obviously, was no prude. Later in life he was to engage in an extended debate with his surprisingly squeamish friend Theodore Roosevelt over the propriety of a mutilation scene in *The Virginian*.[22] Often Wister's friends and critics suggested to him that he smooth some of his accounts of the rougher aspects of Western life. In his later fiction in particular, he would never flinch from the ugliest aspects of Western society. But an unpublished Wister in his mid-twenties up against William Dean Howells was another matter. Perhaps without fully realizing it, Wister had struck the Achilles' heel in Howells's dogmatic Realism—the older man's fastidious desire to publish nothing that a maiden might not read with impunity. When he was older, Wister would be less accepting of Howells's prudish avoidance of the more distressing implications of Realistic writing: "Howells, one timid eye on Mrs. Grundy, was trying to see life steadily and see it whole with the other," Wister wrote in 1930.[23] For a young man, however, sitting at the feet of an established and revered master, the weight of Howells's authority was too great; *A Wise Man's Son* disappeared.

It is pointless to guess what Wister's career might have been had this first major literary effort been published and acclaimed. George Thomas Watkins, who has done the most extensive study of Wister's career, suggests that Howells's rejection was crucial to the development of Wister's art.[24] When Wister turned to fiction again several years later, he did so as a local colorist rather than a social or psychological Realist, and the main goal of his published fiction tends to be a capturing of the "feel" of a place rather than the probing of character. The fiction of Wister's mature years often exhibits a sentimental romanticism which may not have compromised *A Wise Man's Son*. In discouraging the novel, Howells may well have buried a mute, unsung Dreiser. Certainly the Wister who emerged in print in the 1890s was a far cry from the young Realist manqué who took his first novel to the august editor in 1884.

By the spring of 1885, the frustrations of his aborted business career, the unappealing prospect of the law, and perhaps the discouragement over Howells's rejection of his novel were steadily destroying Wister's health, which had never been very good. As a boy he had suffered from weak eyes, chronic headaches, and insomnia, and his years at St. Paul's and Harvard had seen several sieges of a vague but distressing nature, the beginning of a series of strange and elusive attacks that were to last throughout Wister's life. His mother believed that his year in Switzerland in 1871 "undermined his health [and] scarred him emotionally for life."[25] His breakdown of 1885 would send him West for cure. In 1896, he spent the winter in Europe on advice of doctors,[26] and in 1900, he was hospitalized for weeks for a mysterious malady; this was repeated in 1904. In 1908, he complained of "something wrong with my insides that no doctor could name,"[27] and in 1909–10, he was sick for an entire year, mystifying family, friends, and physicians.[28] Eventually, wrote his daughter, these undiagnosed illnesses affected his writing, and "his inability to sustain regular work as an author became a major worry."[29] It is tempting to speculate as to the source of these apparently psychosomatic attacks. The pressures of Wister's childhood might well have produced a psyche unable to accept retreat from responsibility except through the "acceptable" refuge of illness. Further, he inherited from his mother a tendency to extended attacks of probable mental origin—her massive depression of 1869–70 debilitated her for a year in a siege strikingly similar to the one Owen would suffer forty years later.[30]

Whatever the cause, in early 1885, Wister was approaching something very like a nervous breakdown.[31] His father, the doctor, became increasingly worried and wrote privately of his son's "mental illness."[32] Face swollen, eyes blurred, racked by headaches, and plagued by nervous depression, Wister was ready for a change: "In

Philadelphia I sat nibbling at Blackstone in the law office of Francis
Rawle until the Law School should begin a new year in the Autumn;
and now my health very opportunely broke down. I was ordered by
Dr. Weir Mitchell to a ranch of some friends in Wyoming. Early in
July, 1885, I went there. This accidental sight of the cattle country
settled my career."[33]

When he first saw the West in 1885, Wister was not yet ready to
write its story. In fact, superficially he was an unpromising candidate
for the chronicler of the closing of the frontier, yet there were elements in his background that prepared him for that literary role. Although his family was aggressively upper class, it was not typically
aristocratic or genteel, and it deviated sharply from the vacuous norm
of Victorian aristocracy so scathingly sketched by Edith Wharton.

Dr. Wister's dedication to his own work and to his son's career is
most significant, for it was an age in which true gentlemen usually
either did not work at all or maintained a respectable fiction that they
were functioning professionals. Unlike most men of his class, Dr.
Wister took no interest in society and evidently held to a Puritan
work ethic.[34] He was a genuine and thoughtful Episcopalian and an
admirer and pupil of Bronson Alcott.[35] Further, "Dr. Wister was always noted for his wonderful sense of humor, while Sarah seems to
have had little or none."[36] The religion, the romanticism, and the wit
would all be passed on to his son and figure in Owen's fiction.

Sarah Butler Wister was obviously singular. She was an aggressive
woman in an age of female passivity, an opinionated woman in an age
of female vacuity, and a demanding mother in an age when women
coddled their well-bred sons. She zealously promoted the arts and in-
tellect at a time when real concern for such matters was considered a
bit radical, even dangerously outré for people of good family. Her
influence on her son was indelible. Even when he finally married, significantly late in life, a woman "as different from his mother as he
could find,"[37] he still prized strong female character and activism,
praising women who had the courage to "step rather conspicuously
outside of the established convention—the things that a 'lady could
do.' "[38] Sarah Butler Wister did what she wanted, as had her mother
before her.

Fanny Kemble was perhaps emblematic of her grandson's atypical
background. The shadow of her notorious divorce might have "hung
over" other Victorian families, but it seems not to have disturbed the
Wisters. More important, she immeasurably deepened the artistic

heritage of her favorite grandson, Owen. Her charismatic personality, theatrical and musical experience, and cosmopolitan life-style set her far apart from the common run of aristocratic grandparents. She encouraged Owen to write music and poetry; when he was sixteen the two undertook the writing of an opera.[39] Her Continental contacts and her constant traveling constituted a powerful influence on the little boy already unusual in provincial Philadelphian society because of his southern heritage on his father's side. It is hardly surprising that his writing would show a sensitivity to regional distinctions.

All in all, Wister brought an unusual background to the frontier, but not that of a dilettante gentleman "slumming" on the plains. He had unusual intelligence and sensitivity, and he also had a quality critical to the development of his career as a writer—the diffidence of the outsider. The intense little boy, forced early into the arts and bearing the weight of a demanding father, felt perhaps too much the pressure of family and too little overt affection. He was to become a reserved man, always looking carefully at life, but feeling a distance from it. This stance of the neophyte observer, admiringly watching, noting, and recording a way of life to which he was attracted, but from which he recognized his own fundamental alienation, was to become the narrative persona of nearly all Wister's fiction. It was a stance that was the logical outgrowth of a remarkable family. All that was needed was an object for observation, and in the West of 1885, Wister found it.

Wyoming, 1885

The West to which Wister came in June of that year accompanied by two maiden ladies who were friends of his mother was not exactly the "wild West." In five years the territory would be a state. The great days of western migration, when as many as ten thousand wagons a year passed Ft. Laramie on the Oregon Trail, were forty years gone. The last of the great mountain men, Jim Clyman, who had learned his trade with the Rocky Mountain Fur Company before 1820, had died on his California ranch in 1881.[40] Custer had been dead for nearly a decade, and the last hostile Indian chief, Geronimo, was at bay in Mexico. With the Indians gone, the influx of settlers under the Homestead Act swiftly brought an end to the open range; most of the homesteaders in Wyoming arrived on the same spur of the Union Pacific, completed in 1868, as did Wister. Actually, far

from being the miles of empty grassland and wilderness it was a generation before, Wyoming was literally cluttered with cattle, a situation that was shortly to bring hard times. Walter Prescott Webb
writes in *The Great Plains:* "By 1885 the time of reckoning had come.
Overstocking the range had so reduced the grass that either a drought
or a hard winter would bring disaster."[41] Both would occur before
Wister would write his first Western story. In every way, the wide
open spaces had narrowed considerably and the closing of the frontier
was at hand.

This is not to say that Wyoming was as tame in 1885 as, say,
Philadelphia. The Indian uprising of the Ghost Dancers followed by
the massacre of Wounded Knee was still five years in the future, the
last pathetic gasp of the western Indian wars. The limited but thoroughly violent Johnson County cattle war of 1892, in which Wister
would take a personal interest, was yet to come. And all over Wyoming, from the early 1880s until the mid 1890s, the Wyoming
Stock Growers' Association fought a guerrilla war with rustlers and
other libertarian elements inimical to stability and good business.[42]

There was also still plenty of natural beauty and a stunning
amount of space. Overstocked or not, the land was short on people.
Even today, after Alaska and Nevada, Wyoming has the lowest population density in the country, and in the 1880s there were many
fewer people. The Yellowstone, the Grand Tetons, the Wind River
Range, and the mountains around Medicine Bow were virtually un-
inhabited. To the dejected young man who had just crawled down off
his "high, hard stool" it seemed "like Genesis," as he wrote in his
diary.[43]

He wrote a great deal more, although none of it found its way into
print for more than five years. On the train leaving Philadelphia, he
had begun the first of fifteen extensive diaries of his western travels
which would become the source of his fiction. From the beginning,
his eye was good, his appreciation vast, and his commitment to the
West, if not without qualification, strong. On 2 July, he wrote:
"One must come to the West to realize what one may have most
probably believed all one's life long—that it is a very much bigger
place than the East, and the future of America is just bubbling and
seething in bare legs and pinafores here. I don't wonder that a man
never comes back after he has once been here for a few years." On 3
July: "We passed this morning the most ominous and forbidding
chasm of rocks I ever saw in any country. Deep down below, a camp-

fire is burning. It all looked like *Die Walkure*—this which is much more than my most romantic dream could have hoped." On 8 July: "This existence is heavenly in its monotony and sweetness. Wish I were going to do it every summer. I'm beginning to be able to feel I'm something of an animal and not a stinking brain alone." And on 14 July: "I'm a quarter of a century old today."[44] Before another quarter of a century passed, he would write the books that established the West in the popular imagination of America.

Wister spent July and August of 1885 in Wyoming, most of it on the Big Horn Basin ranch of Major Frank Wolcott, a close friend of Amos W. Barber, a former doctor who was the governor of Wyoming Territory and the model for Governor Ballard in several Wister stories. Growing stronger, Wister scribbled in his journal everyday. Already, he was eager to get the West down on paper before it disappeared:

> The details of the life here are interesting. Wish I could find out all about it—and master it—theoretically. It's a life as strange as any the country has seen, and it will slowly make room for Cheyennes, Chicagos, and ultimately inland New Yorks—everything reducted [*sic*] to the same flat prairie-like level of utilitarian civilization. Branans and Beeches [cowboys] will give way to Tweeds and Jay Goulds—and the ticker will replace the rifle.[45]

That was written only ten days after Wister arrived, but already we can make out the concerns that would dominate his fiction—the passion for detail, the fascination with the strangeness of the West and its differences from the East, and the inevitability of this wild, pure land being corrupted by the false values of the East.

It was not only the West itself that fascinated Wister. He realized that the wild country touched a part of his psychology that had been neglected and suppressed. In a letter to his mother, he repeated the line about becoming something of an animal.[46] The West stirred something in him powerfully antithetical to the overly intellectual and hyperrefined character that Sarah Butler Wister had tried to cultivate. For the rest of his life, Wister would be torn between admiration for the spontaneous freedom that the West represented and the lifelong conditioning of his mother. His fiction would reflect this ambivalence—now responding to the "animalism" of the West, now rejecting it.

The trip was the first of fifteen to the West that Wister took between 1885 and 1900, and the journal was the beginning of his career as a writer, although he later claimed he didn't realize it: "Upon every Western expedition I had kept a full, faithful, realistic diary: details about pack horses, camps in the mountains, camps on the sage-brush, nights in town, cards with cavalry officers, meals with cowpunchers, round-ups, scenery, the Yellowstone Park, trout fishing, hunting with Indians, shooting antelope, white tail deer, black tail sheep, elk, bear, mountain sheep—and missing these same animals. I don't know why I wrote it all down so carefully, I had no purpose in doing so, or any suspicion that it was driving Wyoming into my blood and marrow, and fixing it there."[47]

The West was to change Wister's life, but it was to take some time in doing so. The years between 1885 and 1891, when he began writing seriously, were nearly as directionless as the years before. In the fall of 1885, he entered Harvard Law School, where he spent the next three years. He also dabbled in the arts during this time, producing an essay, "Some Remarks on the Greek Play," which was rejected for publication, and an essay, "Republican Opera," which the *Atlantic* published unsigned in April of 1887, but which Wister called "a literary catastrophe."[48] After his graduation from law school, he turned briefly from literature back to his first love, music, and wrote, in 1889, an opera about Montezuma, which he could not get produced.[49] He had by this time accepted a position in the law offices of Francis Rawle, one of the patrician Philadelphia firms. This should have delighted Wister's father, but there is evidence that relations between the two were actually deteriorating, perhaps because Dr. Wister sensed that his son was no more committed to the law than he had been to business.[50]

What Wister did during these years that was significant was to continue his trips to the West. In the summer of 1887, he traveled through British Columbia, Washington, Oregon, California, and Wyoming, gleefully shooting everything that moved and decrying the invasion of the West by eastern tourists.[51] He spent the summer of 1888 wandering the wilderness of Wyoming, often in very rough country and bad weather. In the summer of 1891, he was again in Wyoming, and it was then, his daughter writes, that "his ambition to write Western fiction began to stir. More and more in the following years the Journals became a writer's working notebook."[52] The descriptions of the wilds and the towns, the people and the incidents of his travels were becoming fuller. Some incidents and descriptions as he wrote them were fully formed and needed little conversion into fiction. His description of the abandoned railroad town of Douglass, for example, was the main source for the town of Drybone in *Lin McLean* and other stories, and his account of a rancher gouging out a horse's eye became with little alteration the story of "Balaam and Pedro" and a chapter in *The Virginian*.[53]

The Sagebrush Kipling

If Wister is to be believed, his actual decision to write about the West for publication came suddenly. In *Roosevelt: The Story of a Friendship* (1930), Wister claims it took place, when "one Autumn evening of 1891, fresh from Wyoming and its wild glories, I sat in the club dining with a man as enamoured of the West as I was." The two began to compare experiences. "Why wasn't some Kipling saving the sage-brush for American literature, before the sage-brush and all that it signified went the way of the California forty-niner, went the way of the Mississippi steam-boat, went the way of everything. Roosevelt had seen the sage-brush true, had felt its poetry; and also Remington, who illustrated his articles so well. But what was fiction doing, fiction, the only thing that has always outlived fact." Wister lit up (the claret, he tells us, had been excellent). " 'Walter, I'm going to try it myself. . . . I'm going to start this minute.' " And he claims, by midnight he had written much of "Hank's Woman."[54]

Wister, looking back over nearly forty years, may have exaggerated the drama of this epiphany, but there's no doubt that on the advice of his literary doctor friend, S. Weir Mitchell, he offered "Hank's Woman" and "How Lin McLean Went East" to Henry Mills Alden, senior editor at Harper and Brothers, who accepted the former for the *Weekly* and the latter for the *Monthly*. By January of 1892 Wister was a published author, and he immediately gave up the practice of law for good.[55] He then sent *Harper's* "Balaam and Pedro," a fictionalization of the eye-gouging incident, in early 1893, and Alden rewarded him with a long-term contract under which Wister was to deliver several Western stories over a period of years.

"Balaam and Pedro" was an important landmark for Wister in several respects. Even more than "Hank's Woman," which described squalid lives and a brutal ax murder, this story dealt forthrightly with the seamier side of western life, which Wister and his editor were afraid was "not the kind of thing the general public likes."[56] He published it anyway and, in doing so, put himself four square in the camp of the Realists—led by his old mentor Howells. The story also showed Naturalist leanings, which Wister surprisingly would exhibit often in his career. Even Wister's friend Roosevelt, who had told him "Bully for you!" when he read "Hank's Woman," was distressed by the frankness of "Balaam and Pedro." Roosevelt's criticism of the story and Wister's eventual acceptance of that criticism say much about Wister's literary philosophy and the development of his career. Roosevelt wrote: "I'm perfectly aware . . . that Zola has many admirers because he says things out loud that great writers from Greece down to the present have mostly passed over in silence. I think that *conscientious descriptions of the unspeakable* do not constitute an interpretation of life, but merely disgust all readers not afflicted with the hysteria of bad taste. There's nothing masculine in being revolting. Your details really weaken the effect of your story, because they distract the attention from the story as a *whole,* to the details as an offensive and shocking *part.* When you come to publishing it in a volume, throw a veil over what Balaam did to Pedro, leave that to the reader's imagination, and you will greatly strengthen your effect."[57] Wister did "throw a veil" over the eye-gouging for the 1902 publication of *The Virginian,* and in doing so weakened the story and made the incident, as Philip Durham points out, mystifying.[58] Again Mrs. Grundy, in the unlikely guise of the vigorous T. R., had squelched Wister's Realist instincts.

A happier outcome of the publication of "Balaam and Pedro" was that *Harper's* gave the story to Frederick Remington to illustrate, which he did with a fine painting of Balaam buying the luckless horse from his master while the Virginian looks on. Remington was already known as the country's finest western artist, and his illustration was the first of many for Wister stories in *Harper's* in the 1890s. Amazingly, Wister, who had not met Remington, ran into him by chance before the story was published; they met in the wilds of Wyoming, where the two men were traveling separately. They took to each other, finding they shared, not only an interest in the West and an admiration for each other's work, but a gloomy political philosophy which saw America as a great land being ruined by corrupt politicians and bankers in collaboration with tasteless, valueless immigrants who were debasing the American stock.

This concern with America and "Americanism" dominated much of Wister's thinking in the early 1890s, as is evident in his writing of this period. "Hank's Woman" is about an American who lacks values and proves morally inferior to his European wife, who has them. "How Lin McLean Went East" is really about the creation of the "New American," the westerner, who realizes on a trip to his childhood home in Boston that eastern values have become corrupt and that he has become a native of a better land, the West, with truer standards.

Wister was moving toward an articulation of a vision of America, particularly as embodied in its last and least-sullied frontier, the far West. As early as 1892, he projected an essay to be called "The Course of Empire," which Alden at *Harper's* discouraged because he was afraid it would distract Wister from the fiction that was rapidly developing a popular audience.[59] By early 1895, however, Wister had enough clout to demand reconsideration of the essay, which he had reworked several times and which he now called "The Evolution of the Cowboy." It is one of his most interesting and significant writings, for its encapsulates perhaps better than anything else he ever wrote his philosophy of life and vision of the West.

Wister opens the essay with an account of an English lord and a rough-hewn tourist from Texas eyeing each other balefully on a British train. The toff sees the Texan as crude, and the Texan the toff as a dandy. But, says Wister, they are brothers under the skin. He imagines the Britisher transposed to the frontier, rapidly mastering the skills of riding and roping, already a deadly shot, proving himself a man among men. The point is that both lord and cowboy are fundamentally Anglo-Saxon men, and that racial bond transcends any superficial differences of border and birth (but not breed). Both share an inherent courage, love of adventure, and penchant for romantic action—all transmitted in a direct line from their Anglo-Saxon forebears. The American West, says Wister, is the last free field for Saxonism: "To survive the clean cattle country requires spirit of adventure, courage, and self-sufficiency"[60]—qualities that the cowboys displayed daily and that the lord by virtue of his racial legacy also had, for "deep within him lay virtues and vices coarse and elemental as theirs."[61]

Wister is most emphatic in his claim that the qualities of the westerner are the peculiar province of the Anglo-Saxons, and it is in this essay that we see the first full flowering of his increasingly intransigent racism. Of the cattle country, he says: "You will not find many Poles or Huns or Russian Jews in that district; it stands as yet untainted by the benevolence of Baron Hirsh [Wister's bête noire, the

Jewish banker]. Even in the cattle country the respectable Swedes set-
tle chiefly to farming and are seldom horsemen."[62] One of the healthy
qualities Wister finds in his Saxon cowboys is "the Saxon contempt
for the foreigner," which extends, of course, to native American Indians and Mexicans, two groups that Wister lists with cattle thieves
as constituting the great perils of the plains—the thieves being the
least obnoxious, since they were as daring as the cowboys and often
Saxon as well. The Mexican Wister calls "this small, deceitful alien."

After claiming that the cowboy is a creature straight out of the
Arthurian Middle Ages, Wister reverts to the objective description
characteristic of his early Western stories, and for several pages he
paints a vivid picture of the cowboy, rich with detail and illuminated
by anecdote. He sketches his devil-may-care romanticism, courage,
and fundamental masculinity that meet the challenge of a harsh, demanding job in a harsh, demanding land. As a reporter of local color,
Wister is always effective, and he does well here with the oddities of
western clothing and language and the physical description of western
landscape. Several paragraphs define the "cowpony"—its ancestry, its
spirit, and its indivisibility from its master and his fate. Wister closes
with a nostalgic reflection on the decline of the cowboy, a victim of
modernity in three of its aspects: "the exhausting of the virgin pas-
tures, the coming of the wire fence, and Mr. Armour of Chicago,
who set the price of beef to suit himself. But all this may be summed
up in the word Progress."[63]

Lavishly illustrated by Remington, "The Evolution of the Cowboy"
appeared in the September 1895 issue of *Harper's Monthly* and attracted wide critical comment, most of it favorable.[64] It was the
opening shot in a long campaign of social, political, and historical
essays—some of them book length—which would occupy Wister for
the rest of his life. This was to be Wister's only nonfiction work entirely devoted to the West, but it effectively defined the character of
the cowboy, not only as it was to appear in Wister's own fiction, but
in large degree as it was to become assimilated into American
mythology. Wister establishes in "The Evolution of the Cowboy" the
iconography of the Western—the horse, the gun, the quaint clothes.
He also delineates the patterns of cowboy behavior which were to become commonplace: the solitary asexual existence; the intense, almost
athletic physical activism; the spontaneity; the stoicism and understated acceptance of hardship; the respect for professionalism in any
form; the chivalric ritualization of "code" behavior, whether in treatment of men or women; the profound self-respect.

One aspect of the modern cowboy hero, and of Wister's as he was to appear in *The Virginian,* which did not figure in the portrait painted in "The Evolution of the Cowboy" was a respect for law and order. In the essay Wister makes no bones about the likelihood of finding his Saxon adventurer on the wrong side of the law—his rugged individualism often extending to asserting his right to appropriate other people's property. In the real world of 1895, Wister notes, the cowboy is forced to turn to new ways of wage earning, and as a wage slave "his peculiar independence is of necessity dimmed. The only man who has maintained that wholly is the outlaw, the horse and cattle thief, on whose grim face hostility to Progress forever sits."[65] Given Wister's attitude toward "Progress," this is hardly a condemnation.

As "The Evolution of the Cowboy" indicates, by the mid-1890s Wister had not only found his theme—the vanishing frontier—but he had shaped his attitude toward it. He had already come a long way from the fall of 1891 when his simple intent had been to get the West down on paper as it was and had been before it utterly disappeared. As he wrote his first stories, however, a fuller sense of his fictional calling developed. His original impulse to simple realistic fidelity—the job of the historian and reporter—became augmented in Wister's mind by a need to project the West in romantic terms. The West was becoming for him something like Fitzgerald's vision of unspoiled America at the end of *The Great Gatsby*—a place where man stood "face to face for the last time in history with something commensurate to his capacity for wonder." This tension between realistic and romantic impulses informed all Wister's fiction of the nineties, but nowhere is it more clearly articulated than in the foreword he wrote in 1897 to his friend Remington's first book of drawings: "I have stood before many paintings of the West, . . . the whole mystic and heroic pageant of our American soil; the only greatly romantic thing our generation has known, the last greatly romantic thing our continent holds; indeed the poetic episode most deeply native that we possess. . . . we have a landscape seasoned by mystery, where chiefs and heroes move, fit subjects for the poet."[66]

Western Fiction before *The Virginian*

What Wister felt Remington was doing with paint, he was determined to do with words. By the fall of 1894, he had written enough stories for *Harper's* to fill his first short story collection, *Red Men and*

White. Thinking ahead to the assembling of *Lin McLean* two years later, Wister omitted the Lin McLean stories he had already written. He included two stories of rebellious Indians struggling with long-suffering cavalry troops, "Little Big Horn Medicine" and "The General's Bluff," and a third Indian story, "Specimen Jones," in which Wister's first western character, a colorful vagabond miner, befriends a tenderfoot and outwits a band of murderous Apaches by pretending to be mad. There were two stories of "justice" on the frontier—"The Serenade at Siskiyou," in which the vigilantes of a frontier town lynch a couple of killers to show the bleeding-heart women that evil should not be coddled, and "The Second Missouri Compromise," one of Wister's best stories, in which a wise young governor in the Idaho Territory of 1867—aided by Specimen Jones, now in the army—maneuvers a group of belligerent ex-Confederates into signing a pledge of allegiance to the United States. Another story of lynch law, and one that did not condone kangaroo courts, was "Salvation Gap," about an aging miner who murders his unfaithful mistress and frames her younger lover for the crime, but kills himself in guilt when the lover is lynched.

The final two stories of *Red Men and White* were late additions. Both grew out of Wister's 1894 trip to the Southwest. "La Tinaja Bonita" tells of a Saxon cowboy's rivalry with a Mexican boy for the love of a senorita, but it is more the story of the cowboy's battle with heat and thirst, and eventual madness, in the desert, a sort of southwestern version of "To Build a Fire." "A Pilgrim on the Gila" is utterly different. Wister's most ambitious effort to that time in terms of scope, the story presents a clearly autobiographical narrator who describes scenes of political and social corruption in the Arizona Territory of the 1890s. A host of corrupt characters fill the tale—manipulating politicians, jury-rigging lawyers, payroll thieves, and an apathetic populace that would rather have a law of license than of discipline. This attempt to present a study of society rather than a simple narration points the way to Wister's future efforts.

Red Men and White, published in the fall of 1895, enjoyed modest sales and a respectable critical reception. Two reviews must have particularly pleased Wister. Howells, writing in *Harper's Weekly,* called it "a man's book throughout," and praised Wister's "humorous sense," although he was distressed by "some lingering traits of romanticism."[67] And T. R., in a *Harper's Weekly* review three weeks later, went further, predictably stressing the book's "note of manliness," and calling "The Second Missouri Compromise" "literally a masterpiece."[68]

Lin McLean, which Wister considered his first novel, was largely written by the time *Red Men and White* was published. Its genesis lay in "How Lin McLean Went East," one of those first two stories of the fall of 1891, that initial statement of Wister's vision of the apposition between the jaded, corrupt East and the clean West, and of the westerner as the new American. As more stories of Lin followed, Wister broadened his first extended picture of the cowboy hero. Basically decent, gay, impulsive, not overly bright socially or intellectually but with plenty of common sense and practical competence, physically active, instinctively courageous—the key word for Lin is "natural." He is "nature's gentleman," like Orlando of *As You Like It.*

Wister sandwiched several superficially related episodes together to form the "novel" as it appeared in 1897. Considering that the Western novel is thought of as stressing action, the plot of *Lin McLean* is remarkably tame. The real subject of most of the story is the social maturation of the hero, and in a different setting, its dramatic action would not be far from that of Tarkington's *Seventeen,* just as Lin himself is very like Penrod. Wister opens with "How Lin McLean Went East," an extended sketch of Lin's picaresque life on the frontier of the 1880s, followed by an account of his trip home to Boston, where he decides that his real home is Wyoming. In the next, unrelated episode, back out West, Lin meets, courts, and is luckless enough to win a loud, trashy amazonian waitress who briefly makes his married life miserable until he finds she has been married before and gets rid of her. The book then shifts to a third unrelated story, this originally published as "A Journey in Search of Christmas," in which Lin picks up a street urchin in Denver at Christmas, feeds and pampers him, and eventually adopts the child, who unconvincingly turns out to be the runaway son of the trashy waitress. Finally, Lin meets a decent peasant girl from Kentucky worthy of him. Their inevitable courtship is interrupted when the girl learns of Lin's former marriage and refuses to marry him. Suddenly, however, the ex-wife appears, tells the lovers that they are made for each other, and poisons herself at a dance in a disreputable gambling den. For reasons that are disturbingly vague, this convinces the "true girl" to take Lin back, and they and the orphaned boy live happily ever after.

The novel is rescued from this haphazard plot by the kind of strong descriptive writing in the local-color tradition that saves many of

Wister's early stories. The plains, the mountains, and the deserts of the West are convincing in *Lin McLean,* and Wister's eye for detail and ear for dialogue do not often betray him. The colorful, sometimes grotesque parade of frontier life moves as effectively in *Lin McLean* as anywhere in Wister's writing. The novel, again handsomely illustrated by Remington, was generally well received by the critics, although Wister himself seems to have been aware of its structural weaknesses.[69] In late 1897, however, he was not much concerned with them, for he had decided to marry his cousin Molly—Mary Channing Wister—and for Owen Wister marriage was not a casual thing.

Wister had waited with deliberation until he was thirty-eight to find the right woman, and for the fifteen years of his marriage and the quarter century of his life following her death in 1913 he was convinced that he had. Molly Wister was the obvious prototype of Molly Wood in *The Virginian,* but without the decline in aristocratic fortunes that made the latter a Wyoming schoolmarm. Molly was the cream of Philadelphia society—her Channing blood came from the Brahmin transcendentalist William Ellery Channing—but like Owen her mind set her apart from Main Line stodginess. Genuinely cultured, she was an accomplished pianist, and often played duets with her future husband before their marriage. Although a great beauty and debutante belle in her youth,[70] she worked actively all her adult life helping needy children, particularly in education. At twenty-seven she had been the youngest member of the Philadelphia Board of Education,[71] and when she died the flags of the Philadelphia schools flew at half-mast. In all the massive Wister family correspondence, there is nothing to indicate that Wister did not regard her with a love bordering on worship, as his own father had revered his strong-minded wife, Owen's mother. When she died young, Wister was desolate, and looking back at the end of his life, he still called it "a perfect marriage."[72] Doubtless it was, but when we consider the heroines of *The Virginian* and *Lady Baltimore,* we might wish that Wister had worshiped his goddess less and studied her more before rendering her in prose.

In the summer of 1898, Wister had reached a stopping point in his life. He married in April and seems to have taken most of the rest of the year off. The couple honeymooned, first in Charleston and then in the wilds of Washington state; significantly, each locale was to be the setting of the central love story of Wister's two future novels: the courtship of the Virginian culminates in a honeymoon nominally set in Wyoming, but almost surely patterned after Washington,[73] and *Lady Baltimore* (1906) is a love story set in Charleston.

It was not until the following spring that Wister again attempted fiction, this time a story called "Padre Ignazio," which represented a real departure from his previous work. The story is almost without action, and it shows a psychological depth beyond anything Wister had done previously or was to do again. More important, it was his first fictional departure from the post–Civil War American frontier. The main character of "Padre Ignazio" is a Spanish priest in pre-American California of the early nineteenth century. A cultured man, he finds himself in a cultural desert. A young French-American prospector visits the priest and tempts him to abandon his calling by talking to him of the music the priest is starved to hear, reminding him of the life of the mind. Originally Wister had titled the story "Temptation," and it closes with the padre continuing his errand in the wilderness only after intense inner struggle. *Harper's Weekly* offered the story to Remington to illustrate, but the artist refused, and Wister later claimed in a letter to his mother that he did so because "all the action is in men's minds, and not their bodies."[74]

Wister now wrote quickly other new stories expressly for his second collection, *The Jimmyjohn Boss* (1900). The three new ones—the title story, "Sharon's Choice," and "Twenty Minutes for Refreshments"—were insubstantial fiction, and Wister knew it. "The Jimmyjohn Boss" involves a conflict of wills between a very young but competent trail boss and a camp full of drunken, bestial cowboys; the story is essentially light comedy. The other two are respectively about a children's elocution contest and a baby beauty contest, both painted with lots of frontier local color and southwestern humor. To fill out the overall collection, Wister drew on stories written as far back as his first published work, "Hank's Woman" of 1891. As a whole *The Jimmyjohn Boss* is an uneven gathering and was less well received by the public and the critics than *Red Men and White* or *Lin McLean*. Most reviews concentrated on the accuracy of Wister's picture of western life (generally applauded) rather than any literary merit, and "Padre Ignazio," the most ambitious and subtle story Wister had yet attempted, was particularly singled out for criticism, probably because it was less directly trying to "recreate the primeval West," a literary job that most reviewers now saw as Wister's appointed role.[75]

If Wister was disappointed in the reception of *The Jimmyjohn Boss* he did not show it. He was working during this, the most prolific time of his life, on two unrelated writing projects. The first was a brief biography of Ulysses S. Grant for the Beacon Biographies Series published by Small, Maynard & Company. Wister took on the book at the urging of his friend M. A. De Wolfe Howe, the editor of the series, who was eager to get a study of Grant that would rise above both the muckraking attacks and the fatuous encomia that had characterized commentary on Grant since his controversial presidency. Wister's *Ulysses S. Grant,* published late in 1900, succeeded admirably. Wister, always the realist in his respect for detail, researched his subject exhaustively,[76] and the volume is particularly distinguished for its readable, accurate accounts of Grant's campaigns. Wister chose to disregard completely the unfortunate political years of Grant's life after the Civil War—except for his courageous death—and concentrated on exploring the phenomenon of a common man rising to uncommon heights under pressure. Considering the still-fresh wounds of the war and the florid rhetoric of most writing about Grant at that time, Wister's little book was unusually evenhanded in its qualified appreciation of the general, and it contained some of Wister's best writing; the account of Grant and Lee at Appomattox was widely acclaimed at the time of publication[77] and for years was a commonplace set piece in history books and literary anthologies.

The other project was, of course, *The Virginian.* For years Wister had been working away from his original conception of himself as simply a chronicler of a vanishing world and toward a vision that saw the West in more romantic, symbolic terms. He had been groping in *Lin McLean* toward the development of a character who embodied westernism as the apotheosis of Americanism. But Lin McLean himself had proved too common—and too real it might be added—to support the mythic stature with which Wister wished to endow him. Like Byron seeking to inflate Don Juan, Wister "want[ed] a hero, an uncommon want"; unlike Byron, Wister was unaware of the humor in his puffery. Just before the publication of *The Virginian* in the spring of 1902, Wister wrote Oliver Wendell Holmes, Jr., "I set out to draw a man of something like genius—the American genius."[78]

Despite Wister's wish for integrity of character and theme, *The Virginian,* like all his books of fiction except *Lady Baltimore* (1906), was a scissors-and-paste job. Some seven published stories, the first, "Em'ly," appearing in *Harper's* in November of 1893, were folded into the final novel. Wister had been moving seriously toward production of the full-length work since the spring of 1900 when he wrote and published "The Game and the Nation," that crucial central section of *The Virginian* enunciating Wister's elitist philosophy and proposing the Virginian as a symbol of "the quality": "All America is divided into two classes—the quality and the equality. . . . we decreed that every man should have equal liberty to find his own level. By this very decree we acknowledged and gave freedom to true aristocracy, saying, 'Let the best man win, whoever he is.' Let the best man win! That is America's word. That is true democracy. And true democracy and true aristocracy are one and the same thing."[79]

In the winter of 1901–2 the Wisters, now with three children, moved to Charleston, where they had honeymooned. Wister worked steadily, but although he had the form and development of the book clearly in mind, producing a creative work of the magnitude of a novel clearly strained his limited powers. "My book is like going up a mountain," he wrote his mother in February. "Each time I think I have reached the last rise another unfolds."[80] But by March *The Virginian* was finished; by May it was a best-seller; by the fall it had changed Wister's life irrevocably.

Chapter Two

Beyond *The Virginian*

After *The Virginian*

The publication of *The Virginian* in April of 1902 was the high-water mark of Wister's life in every way. The book was an immediate, smashing success—such a success that for the rest of his life, whatever else he might do, Wister would always be the man who wrote "the book." It was reprinted fourteen times in eight months,[1] an unprecedented public acceptance for an American novel, and by August sales were over a hundred thousand copies. All the reviews were not laudatory—Wister drew fire from some Realist critics[2]—but the vast majority of them were. More important to Wister, the novel was written of as a work of art rather than a cowboy story. The review that probably meant the most to him was a private one: his old friend Henry James wrote of the book, "Bravo, bravo," and of the character of the Virginian, James said, he is "so clearly and finely felt. . . . you have made him *live* with a high but lucid complexity."[3] James may have exaggerated his appreciation out of deference to his long friendships with Wister's mother and grandmother,[4] but his keen critical mind was not one given to tempering judgment for affection's sake.

Less sublime, but in many ways more important, was the financial independence *The Virginian's* popularity brought. "It made money, actual money;—an agreeable experience, wholly new for its author," Wister wrote.[5] Although obviously he was never impoverished and had always lived well and moved in rich company, he had nonetheless never been really financially self-sufficient. Although his writing before *The Virginian* had been successful by the standards of the time, no one in turn-of-the-century America lived elegantly from writing alone, and Wister's income from his law practice was limited by agreement with his firm, since he wrote instead of practicing. His mother was his real source of income, and although she was generous, continued financial dependence in middle age rankled.[6] *The Virginian* ended that; even at the end of his life Wister smugly noted that the novel was selling better than thirty thousand copies a year.[7] It had made him a rich man.

He had other reasons to be satisfied. He and Molly were totally devoted. "I hardly knew the meaning of the word thankful until I began my life with you," she wrote him in 1903,[8] and his letters to her express the same passionate devotion that his father's letters to his mother showed a generation earlier. Wister took enormous satisfaction in their three children, and the couple was increasingly caught up in a glittering social and civic life that put them at the very center of important activity, not only in Philadelphia, but in the country. Molly's work with the school board was gratifyingly producing reforms in education for the poor. Wister was receiving flattering overtures from the Republican party about a potential career in politics. Socially, the Wisters were flying high. In January of 1903, they spent several days at the White House as guests of the Roosevelts. Oliver Wendell Holmes, Jr., and his wife came for dinner, too. Wister recalls, "We all knew each other very well; in the midst of the excellent talk and laughter, the President in sheer joy suddenly put both his hands on the table, bowed over [us] and exclaimed, 'Oh, *aren't* we having a good time!' "[9]

Wister should have been having a wonderful time during these halcyon years, but he wasn't. In her memoirs of the Wister family, his daughter calls the whole first decade of the twentieth century "The Difficult Years."[10] Success notwithstanding, Wister seems to have been miserable most of the time. His letters project a profound and restless discontent. Some of it, of course, may have simply been the well-known psychological letdown that often afflicts writers after a major success: Melville sank into despair on finishing *Moby-Dick,* and Ross Lockridge killed himself while *Raintree County* topped the best-seller lists.

Certainly Wister experienced some kind of writer's block. In the winter of 1902–3, he tried repeatedly to dramatize *The Virginian,* but he couldn't. It was the heyday of Belasco melodrama, and *The Virginian's* popularity made a stage version obligatory.[11] Wister's command of dialogue had always been good, but in a script he was unable to fall back on extended lyric description of landscape or rambling philosophic meditation, his substitutes for effective transition in fiction. Finally he gave up and asked his friend Kirk LaShell, who had experience with adaptation, to dramatize *The Virginian.* The play wasn't

very good, and the critics hated it, but like the novel—or because of
it—it sold and captured the public imagination. Of the play, Wister
later wrote that it was "heartily damned by the New York critics, ran
for a while in non-Broadway, for ten years on the road, is still played
in stock after twenty-seven years, and has been three times filmed,
and once translated."[12]

In 1903, when the play of *The Virginian* went on the road, Wister
went with it. The singularity of his decision to tour with the company may not be immediately evident. It was common enough for
Victorian playwrights to travel with the touring companies of their
plays, tinkering with scripts, experimenting with staging, and soak-
ing up atmosphere in the tawdry but exciting world of the itinerant
theater. Often the writer would try a stint of acting itself—Eugene
O'Neill was to live this sort of life some fifteen years later. But Wister was no Bohemian, slumming with show folks and rubbing elbows
with hoi polloi, while perfecting his craft and experiencing thrills.
He was a middle-aged Philadelphia gentleman, a pillar of the community with a family and a substantial position in the world. Moreover, he was eminently proper, and the turn-of-the-century theater
notoriously was not. What then drove him to go on the road with
the play, traveling from tank town to tank town with a motley crowd
of actors and publicists and a play that he had not even written?

A simplistic answer is that the theater was "in his blood." Fanny
Kemble's influence was undoubtedly still strong, although she had
been dead ten years. Then there had been the Hasty Pudding Club
productions, particularly *Dido and Aeneas,* which Wister repeatedly
tried to stage as a commercial production.[13] In the 1880s he had tried
playwriting often, including the aborted *Montezuma,* and in 1923 he
would finally see the production of *Watch Your Thirst,* a full-length
comedy lampooning the temperance movement. And, of course, there
had always been a stagy quality about even his best fiction—what
Howells hated in Wister's writing and called "the 'blue fire' of melodrama, akin to the theatre."[14]

But traveling with the play accounted for only a small part of Wister's absence from home during these troubled years. While Molly
stayed in Philadelphia or at the family's summer place (usually Avon-
by-the-Sea or Bay Head, New Jersey), her husband encamped here
and there around the East, frequently for weeks or months at a time:
Hot Springs, Virginia; Beaufort, South Carolina; Saunderstown,
Rhode Island. In 1906 he spent six weeks in England with his

mother, but not Molly. These wanderings ended only in 1909—interestingly after his mother's death the previous year—when Wister was stricken with the most dramatic of his chronic illnesses, a mysterious fever that defied diagnosis and confined him to bed for nearly a year.[15]

The disease was only the apotheosis of a series of afflictions that characterized this unhappy period. He seems constantly to have been resting, recovering, marshaling his limited strength, slipping back. The family letters are obsessive about health—mainly Wister's, but also that of Molly and the children. It was a sickly family. Molly was already showing the frailty that would lead to her decline and early death, and of the children she wrote, "I know it seems to you as if our babies were sick more than any others."[16]

The trouble writing, the constant absence from home, the poor health—all were part of a general pattern of deterioration. The extended, restless, sickly depression that drove him West in 1885 seems to have returned with a vengeance after the success of *The Virginian,* and the rest of the decade was "sicklied o'er with the pale cast of thought" and declining creative powers. Little wonder that Wister's only major literary effort of this period was *Lady Baltimore,* of which a recent critic says aptly, "Its pessimism is as pervasive as anything written by Herman Melville or Henry Adams."[17]

Significantly, the book was not about the West. Although Wister worked desultorily during this time on a few stories that would be collected in 1911 in *Members of the Family,* "he 'swapped skies' often, writing political, biographical, and occasional essays as well as stories concerning various aspects of life in America's increasingly urban East."[18] His friendship with Remington cooled markedly, because the artist remained dedicated to portraying the primitive West of his and Wister's youth. Remington didn't appreciate the "civilized" cowboy of *The Virginian,* much less Wister's political and social analysis, increasingly praising decorum and rejecting rootlessness. When Remington died suddenly in 1910, *Collier's* asked Wister to write a tribute to his old friend, but Wister only gave the magazine permission to reprint the last four paragraphs of the 1902 introduction Wister had done for Remington's collection, *Done in the Open.*

Besides *Lady Baltimore,* Wister's only other major work of this period was a book-length biography, *The Seven Ages of Washington,* published late in 1907. His short biography of Grant in 1901 for the Beacon Biographies Series had been well received, and Wister's inter-

est in history, always strong, intensified as his attention turned away
from the West to political and social concerns of the country at large.
In early 1907, the University of Pennsylvania asked Wister to be
their Washington Day speaker, and he gladly accepted; along with
the invitation went an honorary Doctor of Laws. The speech was a
thundering success; Wister received a standing ovation from the audience, from "those dear old Philadelphians who sometimes it is hard
to move," as a witness reported.[19] Driven by the impetus of the re-
search on Washington that he did for the talk, Wister pushed on and
finished *The Seven Ages of Washington* before the year was over.

The biography was a good one—graceful, thorough but not pon-
derous, admiring without being fawning. If crude, plebeian Grant
had been an odd choice for Wister's first biography, this was a con-
genial one. Washington was a more restrained and conservative figure, socially and politically, than many of the young Virginian
firebrands who surrounded him (not to mention northern madmen
like Sam Adams, who must have horrified Wister). The image of
Washington—the cool, responsible aristocrat reluctantly but firmly
grabbing the authoritarian reins when called—pleased Wister, and
this rich American Cinncinnatus did not do manual labor behind his
own plow, either. The subject lured Wister temporarily from his
slump and revitalized him before he sank back into another slough of
despond.

The protracted illness of 1909, so much longer and more serious
than the parade of ills that preceded it, frightened Wister. With
Pope, he must have grown weary of "this long disease, my life." By
the spring of 1910, he had written virtually nothing of importance
in nearly three years. He had been constantly sick, listless and depressed most of the time, and worst of all, he had bcome a perpetual
burden to his wife and family. The Wister's letters from this time
paint a grim picture of what their lives had become. Their daughter,
Fanny Kemble Wister, was by then old enough to remember family
life, and she summarized it years later: "It is hard to see not only
how Molly could have endured it despite her boundless strength but
how she could have gone on holding her family together without him
for weeks and months, nursing him herself much of the time in
1909, and being the never-tiring spearhead and keystone of the Civic
Club. He could not sustain his roles of author, husband and father
for any length of time, while she fulfilled her roles of wife and mother

magnificently and her mandatory duties in her chosen career for civic betterment."[20]

With hindsight it seems obvious that Wister's problem in 1910 was little different from the depression twenty-five years earlier. Perhaps the similarity of the afflictions suggested the cure to Wister—a return West. Henry James came to visit in May, and Wister told him of a plan to go back to Wyoming, to the "curative regions,"[21] for as long as it took to get well. He was hoping for the kind of regenerative transformation that had saved him in 1885. In some degree, he got it.

In August of 1910, now well enough to travel and enormously excited at the prospect of relief from his long misery, he went alone to a cabin in Ishawooa in northwest Wyoming.[22] He stayed there for months, despite Molly's entreaties to return. He wrote her: "No; I shall not come home. . . . it is plain to me that my business is to get well. I can be of no use to you or any one until I do, and until I am able to take up my profession again and publish something important, I shall be blue and without peace of mind."[23] Peace came dropping slow, but it came. In a couple of months, he was walking miles everyday and fishing and riding for hours. More important, the West revived his sensitivity as it had years before. At the end of September, a lyrical letter to Molly describes the country in his old romantic style: "The scene is like a good deal of Lohengrin,"[24] recalling his description of the Wagnerian scene in his first journal. In December he came back to Philadelphia, ready to work.

By the spring of 1911, he was working again, finishing a story and writing two new ones for his next collection of Western tales, *Members of the Family,* published by Macmillan in the fall. A long bittersweet preface to the volume indicated that although the West had worked its magic on him again, his real attitude toward it as he grew older was primarily one of pained nostalgia. "Time steps in," he wrote, "between the now that is and the then that was with a vengeance; it blocks the way for us all; we cannot go back."[25] The tone of romantic contemplation of a lost and better past dominates the book. "What was this magic that came in through the window? . . . as if the desert whispered: Yes, I look as if I were here; but I am a ghost too, there's no coming back. . . . my heart ran over with homesickness for what was no more, and the desert seemed to whisper: It's not I you're seeking, you're straining your eyes to see yourself—you as you were in your early twenties, with your illusion that I, the happy hunting-ground of your young irresponsibility, was going to be permanent."[26]

Members of the Family is a short collection of eight slender tales, none of them among Wister's most distinguished. Four of them— "Happy-Teeth," "Spit-Cat Creek," "Extra Dry," and "Where It Was"—reintroduces a character from *The Virginian,* Scipio Le Moyne, presented here in his wilder, younger days. In three of the stories— all but "Where It Was"—Scipio uses cunning to outwit a trio of frontier con men—a corrupt Indian agent in "Happy-Teeth," the scurrilous peddler/thief Uncle Pasco (whom we remember from "The Jimmyjohn Boss") in "Spit-Cat Creek," and a bunko artist who runs a dishonest shell game in "Extra Dry." In "Where It Was" he is simply the narrator of a treacly tale of young love softening the hard hearts of two old sourdoughs in the Washington Territory. Throughout, Scipio is a colorful character—rascally, garrulous, much-married, and vivid of speech, but also exhibiting the classic Wisterian virtues, which are essentially all the points of the Boy Scout law except "thrifty," "clean," and "reverent."

Of the other stories in *Members of the Family,* only one stands out, "The Gift Horse," which tells of a taciturn young cowboy whom the narrator befriends despite strong hints from other cowboys that there are shady aspects to the man. The friendship nearly costs the narrator his life when the cowboy gives him a stolen horse, and he is almost lynched as a horse thief by a vigilante gang that does hang his friend. The longest story in the book, "The Gift Horse," effectively develops several of Wister's ongoing motifs—the paradox of good and evil existing in one character, the loss of innocence implicit in gaining true knowledge of the West, and the opposition between appearance and reality. It is the one story in *Members of the Family* that completely transcends pathetic sentimentality.

Wister's sense of his lost youth was not so painful but that when the summer of 1911 came he packed up the family and took them back to Wyoming to rough it for three months. It was the first vacation the family had spent together, and Wister enjoyed it so much that during the winter he bought a 160-acre ranch in Jackson Hole and returned in the spring with Molly and the four oldest children. The two summers were idyllic and likely the happiest time in Wister's life.

In the fall of 1912 he was full of energy. The family was back at Butler Place, inherited at Sarah Butler Wister's death in 1908. Wister was writing a new novel, this time about Philadelphia and its society.[27] It was never published, but we may imagine a Philadelphian version of *Lady Baltimore,* perhaps with neither the racism nor the outsider's gawky adulation that compromised that novel. Wister knew the city better than any other writer, and he might have given American literature a fictional Philadelphia to rival Wharton's New York or Marquand's Boston.

In the fall of 1912, though, any time spent writing was time stolen from politics. Wister was running actively for the city council on a reform plank. He was also a passionate supporter—as passionate as it was possible for him to be publicly—of Theodore Roosevelt's Bull Moose candidacy. When Roosevelt came to Philadelphia, Wister took him around, introduced him to a mass rally, and shared the platform with him repeatedly.

Wister fit awkwardly into the hoopla of Progressive politics. He and Roosevelt had their differences—race was one, and Roosevelt's flamboyant style must have grated on Wister at times—although these paled beside the strength of the old boy Harvard ties and years of friendship. Moreover, the conservative wing of the Republican party had fallen firmly into the clutches of manipulative money, Wall Street, and big business. For Wister, Senator Nelson Aldrich of Rhode Island, the voice of Republican big money, was as "yellow rich" as Augustus Belmont, Thomas Fortune Ryan, or Jay Gould, the nouveau riche powers in the Democratic party.

Roosevelt lost and Wister lost with him, but the concern with political issues was to last the rest of his life. He had always been active in city affairs; now the election of 1912 turned him to national issues. Within the next few years, the shadow of World War I would direct his attention beyond America, and his next three books would concern the international crisis. He published no fiction for more than ten years.

If the election loss was a blow to Wister, he did not show it. He was still active, still writing. During the winter, he worked on the Philadelphia novel, and when the summer came, instead of going back to Wyoming, the family moved into their new, big summer house at Saunderstown, Rhode Island. Molly Wister, never physically strong, was pregnant again, and for the first time it was Owen who took care of her. She was forty-three and had been in bad health for a year, but there is no indication that Wister expected serious problems.

In August, Molly died giving birth to the couple's sixth child, a girl. Wister was absolutely desolated. It may be hyperbole to say of most men that they never recover from the loss of a wife, but of Wister it was true. His life stopped cold, and his remaining quarter-century has the air of a muted coda. Four months after her death, at the start of the new year, he wrote in his diary: "The strange feeling came over me that to-day I had begun the final volume of my life. It really began on August 24, 1913. No matter how many chapters it contains, it is in truth the final volume. And the thought is not unwelcome."[28]

The novel about Philadelphia simply disappeared.[29]

"The Final Volume of My Life"

If the end of 1913 was horrible for Wister, 1914 proved worse. Prostrated by the death of Molly, he could get no work done. In January, his cousin and close friend, S. Weir Mitchell, the novelist, died.[30] In the summer, Wister traveled to an inflamed Europe on the brink of war, visiting the ailing Henry James at Lamb House for a few days in July and returning to America just before the battles of August. In the fall, his old friend and traveling companion Agnes Irwin, who had consoled him greatly after Molly's death, also died. The European situation depressed him deeply. On the last day of 1914, he wrote: "When has the world known a year more terrible than this . . . ? There is none in the whole recorded memory of mankind. I am glad that those I have lost who were dear and dearest did not live to see it. Will 1915 be any worse? It may very well be much worse. I have but small hope it will be better."[31]

For Wister, though, 1915 *was* better. Terrible as he found the war, he was spurred to write. In November of 1914, he published a small article on his travels before the war, which he noted was his first on a European subject.[32] Early in 1915, Wister had been invited to address the graduation of Trinity College, now Duke University. For the occasion he worked and reworked his reactions to the war and his German travels before it. His sorrow at the war and his outrage at Prussian destruction of European culture grew from a short speech to a small book, becoming an extended plea for American intervention. More than anything the volume, eventually titled *The Pentecost of Calamity* and published first in the *Saturday Evening Post* and then by Macmillan (1916), reveals the unhappy state of Wister's mind. He had always had great admiration for German culture and order, and his lifelong touting of "Saxon" virtues inclined him to accept propaganda about German racial superiority. But he could not deny the ugly reality of Prussian brutality and bigotry. For Wister, the moral failure of Germany was emblematic of the crisis of Western civilization.

The Pentecost of Calamity was Wister's opening gun on behalf of a cause that was to occupy him for several years. After 1915, he became increasingly an outspoken advocate of the Allied interests in the war, and a vitriolic critic of any voices opposed to that cause. A particular bête noire was Woodrow Wilson, whose 1916 campaign slogan, "He Kept Us Out of War," Wister thought disgraceful, and whom he repeatedly attacked in articles and public letters. He even published a poem in the Springfield *Republican,* invoking the wrath of America's forefathers upon Wilson's beleaguered head: "But if its fathers did this land control / Dead Washington would wake and blast your soul."[33] If this wasn't one of Wister's more distinguished efforts, his carefully timed pre-election article in *Colliers,* "If We Elect Mr. Wilson," was less sophomoric. It didn't help lead to a Wilson defeat as Wister hoped, but the tide of public opinion in favor of intervention was swelling, and Wister was on the side of the angels.

America's declaration of war in April of 1917 was immensely satisfying to Wister, but it did not end his efforts for his now-expanded cause, that of Anglo-American friendship. In November of 1918, he published a long essay in *American* magazine, "The Ancient Grudge," accusing America of misspent years of Anglophobia and pleading a commonality of interest in the Atlantic community. The end of the war shortly after only intensified Wister's desire to promote English-American relations. In early 1919, he sailed for an extended trip to England, and two years later a fuller version of his article appeared as *A Straight Deal or the Ancient Grudge* (1921), a book urging America and England to bury the hatchet if they had not already done so through cooperation in the war.

Wister was then at work on a much longer, and much more subtle, statement on World War I, *Neighbors Henceforth* (1922), an elaborate personal essay looking back upon the carnage and devastation of the war, probing the rubble and shoring the fragments against ruin, questing for hope and meaning in disaster. Wister reviews at length, largely through vignettes, both the horror of the war and its moments of nobility. He comes to the unsurprising conclusion that it had not all been in vain, that the war had produced an elevation of spirit in response to crisis that could inspire mankind to carry on. At well over four hundred pages, *Neighbors Henceforth* was the most ambitious writing Wister had attempted in the twenty years since the success of *The Virginian,* and the effort must have been considerable. He was past sixty now, with a lifelong history of poor health and difficulty writing, but the need to respond to the horror of the war seems to have called forth reserves that the challenge of writing fiction could not. *Neighbors Henceforth* is neither profound nor memorable, but it is a well-written and moving testament to the attempt of a sensitive mind to wrestle with the enormity of disaster in a chaotic world.

The decade following the outbreak of the war found Wister writing more than just political commentary and the quasi-philosophical trilogy formed by *The Pentecost of Calamity, A Straight Deal or the Ancient Grudge,* and *Neighbors Henceforth.* As his mother had a half century earlier, he became concerned about what he saw as the declining intellectual and artistic standards in America. In June 1915, he published an acerbic article in the *Atlantic,* "Quack Novels and Democracy," accusing what he called the "genteel" American critics of lack of toughness in their criticisms of popular literature, particularly fiction, and saying that they thereby encouraged the production of trash. The article was written in support of Edward Garnett's 1914 *Atlantic* diatribe, "Some Remarks on American and British Fiction," and it kicked off a long literary debate on the quality of American fiction that involved most of the country's major critics. The statements and rebuttals lasted well ino the 1920s; they culminated in Sinclair Lewis's Nobel Prize acceptance speech in 1931, defending the new realism against the old romanticism[34] and belligerently claiming for the new generation of American writers the recognition that aging Owen Wister had accorded them a decade or more earlier.

Ironically, and very much to his credit, the curmudgeonly Wister had for a long time appreciated and encouraged the best, and often the most disturbingly iconoclastic, of the younger writers. Far from accepting his friend Roosevelt's cavalier dismissal of Zola and the Naturalists, Wister had admired Crane, London, and Garland back into the 1890s when patrician taste favored F. Marion Crawford.

Writing to Richard Harding Davis after the death of Frank Norris he commented, "He seemed destined to do—almost anything. The loss of Norris is heavy and real."[35] In the 1920s, he became an early and emphatic supporter of Hemingway, whom he met in Wyoming and Paris, where he read the rough draft of *A Farewell to Arms,* praising it effusively and telling Hemingway, "Don't touch a thing!"[36] When Hemingway was short of money, Wister sent him an unsolicited check for five hundred dollars and said of the younger writer, "If I were thirty, that's the way I should wish to write."[37] Hemingway reciprocated the admiration, both personal and professional, and late in his life, he wrote of Wister, "He was the most unselfish and most dis-interested [gentleman] and the most loving."[38] To the end of his life, Wister continued writing and campaigning for the younger generation in fiction. In 1936, he was active, along with Wilbur Cross and Eugene O'Neill, in a small group that proposed Sinclair Lewis for membership in the American Academy of Arts and Letters; when Lewis was refused, Wister continued to press for his eventual acceptance the following year.[39] Hemingway wrote of him, "He does, personally, seem to belong to the same generation as we do."[40]

In 1924, after having written no fiction for nearly a decade and a half, Wister abruptly began work on stories about the West again. The 1920s in general seem to have been an Indian summer for him, a period of some spiritual and intellectual recovery after Molly's death and before the incapacity of old age. He began the decade with *A Straight Deal* and the lengthy *Neighbors Henceforth,* a book that drew from him the greatest sustained productivity of his life; he would finish the period writing the substantial *Roosevelt: The Story of a Friendship* (1930), his last book. In 1924, he moved from the Center City Philadelphia house he had shared with Molly to Bryn Mawr, his Philadelphia address for the rest of his life. There he wrote the stories that eventually made up *When West Was West* (1928).

The nine stories that Wister collected in 1928 for his last book of fiction were even more wistful and nostalgic than those of *Members of the Family,* published seventeen years earlier. Seven of the nine end in pathos, if not genuine tragedy, and the world of this fiction is consistently bleak. The characters are a grim lot: degenerated and abused Indians whose land and dignity have been stolen, aging pioneers who have seen the West turn from a Garden of Eden to a blighted junkyard filled with cheap people and their cheap trash, failed idealists unable to impose morality and vision on a brave new world gone

sour. Wister wrote no introduction for the collection, and none was
necessary, for his attitude toward his material was manifest: more in
sorrow than in anger he lamented the passing of America's last real
possibility of fulfilling its dream—the West.

At the center of *When West Was West* are three pessimistic stories
of the Southwest, each an account of how a new "member of the family," Doc Leonard, comes to realize that life in the postfrontier boon-
docks is often nasty, brutish, and short, and that the character and
morals of the inhabitants are correspondingly diminished. The heirs
of the cowboys, mountain men, and pioneers are a Snopesian lot—
hypocrites, cheats, corrupt politicians, ne'er-do-wells, and scurvy
hangers-on. It is as if Trampas had won the famous duel and his get
had inherited the Western earth. In two stories, "Once Round the
Clock" and "Little Old Scaffold," an aged representative of southern
chivalry, Colonel Steptoe McDee, Doc Leonard's mentor, fights a
one-sided battle for control of a Texas county with a murderous quack
doctor and her crowd of assorted degenerates, murderers, and pork-
barrel politicians. McDee eventually wins, but dies in the process,
assassinated, and the reader is sure that some new rough beast will
come along shortly to poison the wells. A third Texas story, "Skip to
My Lou," is one of Wister's ugliest and one of his best. It tells of
Doc Leonard's confrontation with a West Texas town in which the
citizens preach a simpering moral fascism while covertly practicing
prostitution of a singularly depraved variety. Finally, there is "Absalom and Moulting Pelican," a story that is intended as comedy, but
that paints such a bleak picture of life on an isolated Arizona army
post with its heat, boredom, and intellectual stagnation that the dismal setting itself becomes a sort of naturalistic character, as in Garland's *Main-Travelled Roads* or Rolvaag's *Giants in the Earth*. The main
characters, a grotesque minister intent on proving the Apaches one of
the lost tribes of Israel and his protégé, an aging Indian whose whole
tribe has been massacred, are finally simply pathetic.

Three Wyoming stories in *When West Was West*, "Bad Medicine,"
"Lone Fountain," and "The Right Honorable the Strawberries," also
form a thematic group. Wister thought of Wyoming as "his West,"
and he still owned property there, although he had not been back to
the ranch since Molly died, so the setting of these tales is appropriately beautiful in contrast to the blasted Southwest of Doc Leonard's
wanderings. By contrast, the resolutions are all the more depressing.
"Bad Medicine" is the sympathetic study of a dispossessed Shoshone

Indian prince who clings to a measure of dignity until he demeans himself fawning for white attention and then is killed by his own superstition in a freak accident while posing for photographs in Yellowstone Park. "Lone Fountain" tells of a superb trapper and guide, an original mountain man, who falls in love with a fiery Sicilian woman; she communes with nature and is consumed by what appears to the trapper to be an avatar of the god Apollo in the guise of a sudden geyser. He wanders the mountains at the end of the story, an old broken man, seeking other visions that will make him less forlorn, although his first has turned his hair white.

"The Right Honorable the Strawberries" is the longest story of the collection, and arguably the best. It stands as Wister's last major study of the customs, mores, and values of western society, as well as a eulogy for that world.[41] For his main character, an English lord loose on the plains, Wister went back more than a quarter of a century to the 1895 essay, "The Evolution of the Cowboy," in which, as we saw, he claimed a racial and spiritual kinship between the Saxon nobility of England and the cowboys of America. The main character of "Strawberries" is such a creature, and the first part of the story traces his remarkable success in the frontier world. But when a crisis develops, he cracks, slipping into a sordid pattern of gambling, drinking, and cheating at cards. He is finally saved from death by a common cowboy, whom he posthumously acknowledges to have been the better man. The story seems a repudiation of some of the romantic theory that underlay Wister's early Western fiction.

The closing story of *When West Was West* is as patently Wister's *last* Western story as "Crossing the Bar" is Tennyson's *last* poem. "The Sign of the Last Chance" tells of a bunch of old derelict cowboys sitting in a decaying inn a generation or more after the closing of the frontier. They talk, reminisce about the days of old, bewail the squalid quality of their lives. Then they hear a story about the English custom of ceremoniously burying the tavern signs of English pubs when their time had come. As one, the cowboys rise arthritically, troop out, tear down the tavern's sign, "The Last Chance," and bury it.

Wister's time was not quite past, but he would write no more of the West. *When West Was West* was published in 1928 to almost unequivocally excellent reviews. Critics still applauded the realism of Wister's work, and Charles Poore wrote in the *New York Times Book Review* that Wister was "one of the comparatively few writers of

Western tales who seems to know what he is talking about."[42] At the same time, Macmillan issued Wister's collected works in a handsome multiple-volume edition for which Wister wrote introductions and rewrote a few minor scenes in *The Virginian* and other books. His interest in the West, though, was past. He was already working on another subject that he knew even better—his friend, Theodore Roosevelt, now dead for nearly a decade.

The Roosevelt biography grew into a substantial book of nearly four hundred pages in the two years Wister worked on it, but it began as a personal reminiscence. For years Wister had been jotting down notes and journal entries on the prominent men he had known, and in the late 1920s, he began to publish them discreetly, some in the Harvard alumni magazine, some more publicly. In 1928, the *Atlantic* carried a long sketch of Dr. Coit, the venerable headmaster of St. Paul's during Wister's years there.[43] Wister's work on Roosevelt had similar beginnings, but it grew steadily. In early 1929, Wister learned that he was to receive the prestigious Roosevelt Medal, named in memory of the president, awarded to Americans who had made a significant contribution to the writing of history. Wister's citation mentioned his fidelity in capturing the cattle country in fiction as well as his biographies of Washington and Grant, and it may well have spurred him to expand his study of T. R. into a more genuinely historical document.

Wister realized, though, that he was writing as much about himself as about Roosevelt, and his working title throughout was *Roosevelt: The Story of a Friendship*. He dealt almost entirely with his personal relationship with the president from their meeting as undergraduates at Harvard until Roosevelt's death in 1919, delineating Roosevelt's character as well as his own through a parade of stories, letters, and comments. Woven into the book are sketches of a dozen or more prominent Americans, including Roosevelt's "tennis cabinet," who were friends and colleagues of both Roosevelt and Wister—Oliver Wendell Holmes, Henry Adams, Henry Cabot Lodge, Elihu Root, Leonard Wood, and Gifford Pinchot. Taken together, the cast of characters formed the rootstock of America's ruling class at the beginning of the twentieth century, the inner circle of the power elite both of the Republican party and the country. His portraits of Holmes ("An aristocrat in morals as in mind, with a fortunate touch of both Puck and Ariel")[44] and Root ("When he comes there, it will make Purgatory much pleasanter for me")[45] are particularly rich.

At the center of the book stands Roosevelt, and if Wister is not unbiased in his portrait of his complex friend, neither is he entirely adulatory. The Roosevelt who emerges from these pages is predictably a more civilized and sophisticated figure than the "rough rider" of popular history. In Wister's account, Roosevelt's scholarly appreciation of history and literature, his urbane sense of humor, and his courtly command of the written and spoken word overshadow the wide grin and the big stick.

Wister also reveals Roosevelt as a humane figure, a man with considerably more compassion and understanding of all sorts and conditions of people than the haughty Wister. It was Roosevelt, and perhaps only Roosevelt, who could make Wister aware, if not repentant, that his aristocratic principles often left him insensitive to injustice and suffering. Roosvelt took Wister to task for his racism, once attacking *Lady Baltimore* in a six-thousand word letter which accused the author unequivocally: "In *Lady Baltimore* you give what strength you can to those denouncing and opposing the men who are doing their best to bring a little nearer the era of right conduct in the South."[46] Race was always a bone of contention between the two friends, and Roosevelt never gave an inch. In 1916, he wrote Wister that he did not "know a white man of the South who is as good a man as Booker Washington today,"[47] and years earlier, when he had horrified Wister by appointing a black collector of customs in Charleston, he beseeched his friend, "Why goodness me! . . . Why don't you see—why you *must* see that I can't close the door of hope upon a whole race."[48]

It is to Wister's credit that he reported his disagreements with Roosevelt candidly and that he often realized that his Progressive friend saw life more fairly and more broadly when it came to sympathizing with the lot of the common man. Ruminating on Roosevelt's pro-labor sentiments during the trust-busting days, Wister wrote: "I did not live in coal mines or railroad yards; the talk I commonly heard was the talk of powerful people, well-to-do, sheltered by their own ability and the success which it had brought them."[49]

It did not occur to Wister that his class might have been sheltered by more than just "their own ability," but he knew at least that his view of life from Philadelphia's Main Line was a narrow one. He was, after all, seventy now, and his thought was the product of a world long gone. The children were grown, most of his friends dead, and during the 1930s he increasingly traveled in Europe, wandering in and out of cathedrals, visiting old houses, brooding over battlefields. He still wrote now and then—short articles on his friends or people who had touched his life. He did a sketch of his critic friend John Jay Chapman in the *Atlantic* in 1934, an essay "In Homage to Mark Twain" in *Harper's* in 1935, a tribute to William Dean Howells in the *Atlantic* in December of 1937.

In his last years, he seems to have put the West completely out of his mind. His daughter says that he never spoke of it,[50] and when he traveled in his last decade it was always up and down the east coast, or to Paris or London. His last writing was for a projected book on French wines, which was never published.[51] He still spent part of each summer in Kingston, Rhode Island, a quiet and reticent resort in contrast to the vulgarity of Newport, which he despised. He died there suddenly of a cerebral hemorrhage on 21 July 1938. His body was taken to the Laurel Hill graveyard in Philadelphia and buried beside that of Molly.

Chapter Three

Early Western Fiction

Red Men and White

The decade from 1892 to 1902 is the core of Wister's career as a writer—so much so that were we to lose everything he wrote and published after that time, all the important works in terms of artistry and impact would remain. We would still have his four most significant books of Western fiction: *Red Men and White* (1896), *Lin Mc-Lean* (1898), *The Jimmyjohn Boss* (1900), and *The Virginian* (1902). After *The Virginian*, Wister's interests turned away from the West— to social fiction (*Lady Baltimore*, 1906), to his growing family, and to politics and world affairs. He continued to produce a trickle of Western stories through the first decade of the twentieth century, collecting them in 1911 in *Members of the Family*, and then, more than fifteen years later, he had enough stories for a final collection in 1928, *When West Was West*.

Nearly all Wister's work of the 1890s was first published in *Harper's*, where it was edited by his friend and literary mentor, Henry Mills Alden. Starting with "Hank's Woman" and "How Lin McLean Went East" in 1892, Wister published some twenty stories, which eventually appeared as the short story collections, *Red Men and White* and *The Jimmyjohn Boss*, and the "proto-novel," *Lin McLean*. The two collections are uneven, offering both the best and the worst of Wister's early writing, but they are fascinating, both for the picture they give of the West and for the insight they provide into Wister's first working of the raw material he would fashion into *The Virginian*.

Of the two books, the first, *Red Men and White*, is demonstrably the better, although it is harsh to say of *The Jimmyjohn Boss*, as one Wister critic did, that "most of the stories in the collection were second-rate performances."[1] It is perhaps significant, though, that *Red Men and White* in the first edition is far better bound and printed than its successor and that Frederic Remington contributed seventeen fine illustrations to it and only six to *The Jimmyjohn Boss,* published at a time when his friendship with Wister was deteriorating.[2]

With one exception, "La Tinaja Bonita," there are two types of stories in *Red Men and White*—Indian stories and tales of law and order. In each of the first kind—"Specimen Jones," "Little Bighorn Medicine," and "The General's Bluff"—wily, dangerous, semisavages are outwitted and brought to grief by white men. The law and order stories—"The Serenade at Siskiyou," "Salvation Gap," "The Second Missouri Compromise," and "A Pilgrim on the Gila"—are all stories in which malefactors—outlaws, rebels, criminals—are confronted with the civilizing force of authority and society. Throughout, Wister's perspective wavers between a humorous bemusement at the quaint ways of a barbarous people, Indian or white, and a reportorial objectivity toward exciting and sometimes distasteful material. In the latter guise, Wister often comes surprisingly close to the naturalist he might have been had he fallen under the influence of Zola rather than Howells.

"Specimen Jones" can be considered an Indian story because the climax finds the hero, Jones, outwitting a bloodthirsty gang of Apaches, and because the whole action of the story, from the opening description of a tortured miner, is overhung by the threat of the Indians. Specimen Jones, an itinerant miner and saddle tramp, is the first of Wister's many Western local-color "characters." Jones could have walked out of the pages of Bret Harte: cool, laconic, leathery, casually understated, he carries ore samples wherever he goes and sings a great medley of songs in German and other languages.[3] At an Arizona stage stop, Jones befriends J. Cumnor, the first of Wister's tyros. Just arrived from the East and wet behind the ears, Cumnor is the butt of some vicious southwestern humor, including the classic jig dancing to a six-gun fired at the feet. Jones rescues him, and the kid gratefully tags along with the miner, learning the wisdom and etiquette of manhood and survival in a tough land. Finally, trapped by the Indians, Jones and the boy escape by feigning madness, dancing and cavorting in the hot sun until the superstitious savages flee.

"Little Bighorn Medicine" is more purely a story of Indians, and in it we find the classic Wisterian apposition between civilizing authority, in this case the cavalry, and brute, anarchic savagery. An ambitious and arrogant young chieftain of the Crows, Cheschapah, is flexing his muscles and trying to stir up the tribe against a small army garrison. Cheschapah declares himself a medicine man, supplied with seltzer powder and other chemical hocus-pocus by a corrupt feed and grain speculator who stands to profit from an Indian war. Despite the wise counsel of his father Pounded Meat and other tribal elders, Cheschapah manages to incite the young Crow braves to a brief war, and many Indians, including the would-be medicine man, are killed. The chastised Indians realize the error of their ways and submit, sadder but wiser, to the white man's order and justice.

A major character in "The General's Bluff" is General Crook, a real and important Indian fighter of the 1880s. The story is really an extended sketch of one of Crook's campaigns and a study of the operations of his cavalry troop, one of whom is the recently enlisted Specimen Jones, fresh from his Apache adventure. He pops up here and there in the story, saving the troopers from anonymity. The general's "bluff" is outwitting the Indian chief E-egante—also a real person—into thinking that Crook has far more soldiers than he has. There is an interesting subplot about Sarah, an Indian interpreter but the lover of E-egante's youth, who finds herself torn between the security of her marriage to a white man and her primal instincts to return to the freedom of the Indian world. The "primitive" wins out, and she flees dramatically with E-egante.

Of the law and order stories in *Red Men and White,* the most impressive and the most atypical is "Salvation Gap," a tale in some ways reminiscent both of Harte's better and less sentimental mining camp stories and of the psychological probings of Ambrose Bierce. Drylyn, a slow-witted old miner, is cuckolded by his dance-hall girlfriend, The Gazelle, who gives his presents of gold dust to a younger man. Drylyn slits her throat and frames his rival for it. A lynch mob forms, and despite the heroic efforts of the sheriff to reason with them, the miners string up the wrong man. But Drylyn, torn by guilt, suddenly confesses and begs the repentant mob to kill him. When they won't, he stabs himself and, like Tennessee's partner in the Harte story, joins his victim.

"Salvation Gap" is the first of Wister's several treatments of lynch law, and it represents one side of the author's ambivalent feelings on the matter. For the authoritarian Wister, the term *lynch mob* must have implied a certain logical contradiction. Lynching connoted the operation of discipline and justice, if of a rough vigilante kind, but a mob for Wister was always a gang of barbarians. This is an example of the internal tension in Wister between the austere and proper Philadelphian and the business-hating boy yearning for freedom. Wis-

ter's point in "Salvation Gap" is that this group, having lynched the
wrong man, was a "bad" mob of no-account miners and riff raff—
hardly a substantial citizen in the bunch. What Wister wanted was
a "good" mob. He created it in "The Serenade at Siskiyou," a story
that opens with a stage holdup and the ruthless killing of the driver
by a pair of brothers who are soon caught. The sympathetic women
of the town's Ladies Reform and Literary Lyceum, however, take pity
on the two prisoners, comforting them in their cells, and sending
them flowers and imported pound cake. Finally, their husbands, the
good burghers of Siskiyou, mindful particularly of the women's lack
of concern for the dead driver and his family, take matters into their
own hands. The women ask the town band to serenade the murderers
as they leave town for trial, but when the band marches to the jail-
house playing "Fatinitza," they find the prisoners twitching at the
end of ropes surrounded by masked, but ill-disguised townsmen, who
force the band to finish playing before the horrified women and dan-
gling bodies. The most sensible of the women later asks her fiancé if
he was among the men, and then hurriedly and approvingly says,
"Never mind! I don't want to know ever!"[4]

Justice is less well served, in Wister's terms, in "A Pilgrim on the
Gila," the most ambitious story in *Red Men and White*. It begins in
Washington, D.C., where the narrator, bound for Arizona, hears ef-
fusive praise for the scenery and civilization of the area by politicians
proposing the territory for statehood. The reality, however, belies the
romantic fictions of the orators. The narrator finds the state to be
mostly a blighted desert rather than a lush Eden, and the population
so glowingly described two thousand miles away is really a motley
collection of trashy itinerant cowboys, shiftless tramps, and spineless
proles manipulated by venal lawyers and politicians in league with
the even more corrupt local business interests.

To the narrator's horror, the citizenry doesn't even respect the U.S.
Army: "I began to notice how popular sympathy was not only quite
against the United States, but a sentiment amounting to hatred was
shown against all soldiers. The voice of respectability seemed entirely
silent; decent citizens were there, but not enough of them. . . . I
supposed it something local then, but have since observed it to be a
prevailing Western antipathy. The unthinking sons of the sagebrush
ill tolerate a thing which stands for discipline, good order, and obe-
dience, and the man who lets another command him they despise. I

can think of no threat more evil for our democracy, for it is a fine thing diseased and perverted—namely, independence gone drunk."⁵ The narrator is one of several witnesses to a robbery, and the thieves are caught. It looks like the prosecution has an open-and-shut case, but chicanery carries the day. The jury is bought off with the very funds that were stolen, and no one is punished. Wister's narrator concludes by advising the defendants' dishonest lawyer that he can look forward to a fine career in politics.

The one story in *Red Men and White* that is nearly completely comic is "The Second Missouri Compromise," a tale set in Boise, Idaho, just after the Civil War. The new territory finds itself with a state legislature largely composed of unregenerate Confederate veterans, led by "characters" Powhattan Wingo and F. Jackson Gilet. These are courtly but violent southern gentlemen, full of Ciceronian rhetoric, a festering resentment of the North, and a chip on the shoulder over the injustices of the war. They have been summoned for a session of the legislature, but the funds to pay them have not yet arrived, to the great concern of young Governor Ballard, an isolated northerner and another of Wister's symbols of competence. Stalling for time, Ballard announces that he is withholding the pay until the legislators have signed a loyalty oath to the United States government, an oath most of them fled the South to avoid. Things grow ugly, but Ballard has secretly called for the intervention of the small local garrison of cavalry, and who should turn out to be the leader of a rescue detachment but Trooper Specimen Jones. Jones, competent himself, realizes the ticklishness of the situation and prudently arrests Ballard and the state treasurer who guards the empty strongbox from which the pay is expected to come. The tension is broken. Eventually the money comes, and the ex-Confederates sign the oath to get it. Order and judgment prevail, and Specimen Jones is promoted to become "the Singing Sergeant."

"La Tinaja Bonita" is the only story in *Red Men and White* that concerns neither Indians nor order. Although it develops one of Wister's earliest love plots, it is essentially the story of man against nature, a bit like Stephen Crane's "The Open Boat" or Jack London's "To Build a Fire." The hero, an American named Russ Genesmere, is jealously in love with a flirtatious Mexican girl, Lolita. Teasing a young Mexican boy, she arouses Genesmere's suspicions, preparing him for a rush to judgment like Othello's. He forces himself to cross a particularly dangerous, waterless stretch of Arizona desert to reach Lolita and confirm his fears. Wister effectively delineates the process of Genesmere's mental and physical deterioration in the sun. Staggering to the *tinaja bonita* ("good spring") near her home, he finds her there innocently with the Mexican boy, but in his delirium, he imagines them to be guilty and stabs the girl. She dies by his side, and he, now parched beyond saving, dies too. They are buried together.

For the most part, Wister was pleased with the critical reception of *Red Men and White*, although he resented being thought of as a teller of "Western tales," since the genre had no great tradition of distinction. The *Atlantic* paid tribute to Wister's powers as a Realist, noting a "confusion of the real and the actual," but saying in sum, "the book is so strong in its graphic lines, so dramatic in its scenes, so full of splendid health."[6] The reviews uniformly recognized the two great strengths of Wister's Western writing: "Wister described the West with accuracy, and he was clever at characterization."[7]

The Jimmyjohn Boss

Wister's second collection of stories written during the 1890s was *The Jimmyjohn Boss and Other Stories* (1900). Thematically it is more uneven than *Red Men and White*, although Ben Merchant Vorpahl, whose *My Dear Wister* is the best study of the writer during this period, claims that "historical continuity rather than atavistic survival comprised the book's focus."[8] It is certainly true that much of the material in *Red Men and White* was informed by a concern for "atavistic survival," and to a considerable degree the book was an exercise in realism strongly colored by Naturalistic treatment. Life-and-death struggles between men in various social relationships are at the heart of every story except "La Tinaja Bonita," in which the deadly rivalry between men is ancillary to an even more deadly struggle to survive a hostile nature.

It is harder to agree, though, that *The Jimmyjohn Boss* is truly informed by "historical continuity," for it is as eclectic as anything Wister wrote, a random gathering of all his Western fiction not included in *Red Men and White*, *Lin McLean*, or the forthcoming *The Virginian*, much of which Wister had written by 1900. In fact, the first story in *The Jimmyjohn Boss*, "Hank's Woman," was Wister's first published story, dating back to 1892 in *Harper's*. If *The Jimmyjohn Boss* has continuity, it is only in its diversity. The stories exhibit all the major themes of Wister's early Western fiction: the exaltation of competence; the initiation of the neophyte; the establishment of the immediacy of place projected through realistic but eccentric detail; the inherent apposition of superior and inferior races, classes, and individuals; the essentially sordid nature of much of humanity and most lives; the grotesque and comic character of day-to-day life in a strange new western world.

Surely, *The Jimmyjohn Boss* is a more comic collection overall than *Red Men and White,* although it contains two stories that are unquestionably pathetic and that border on genuine tragedy—"The Promised Land" and "Hank's Woman." There is a casual quality to the other stories, except "Padre Ignazio," and three of them mark Wister's first attempts at pure comedy. All told, the book is a light effort, and Wister, buried deep in writing *The Virginian,* was evidently little disturbed by the lukewarm reception *The Jimmyjohn Boss* received.[9]

The title story is a classic rite-of-passage account of a young man's triumphant trial by fire, and it is also a typical Wister tale of the quality mastering the *canaille.* The hero, Dean Drake, is very young—nineteen—but very competent. An orphan, "since the age of twelve he had looked out for himself . . . getting along in his American way variously, on horse or afoot, across regions of wide plains and mountains, through towns where not a soul knew his name."[10] "Young Drake he is a goot one," says his German-American employer, cattle king Max Vogel, and that seems to be the consensus of everyone who meets the boy. To test his protégé, and because there are never enough good men, Vogel sends Dean into the mountains to boss his toughest trail camp, a camp that has already broken the will of seasoned foremen. Will the crude and sometimes brutal cowboys yield to the will of a physically slight "boss" scarcely old enough to shave? Deciding that keeping the men from liquor is crucial to discipline, Drake rests his authority on a temperance edict, which is violated on Christmas when a scheming peddler, Uncle Pasco, smuggles in a demijohn. Outgunned and overpowered, Drake first watches the drunks break up the camp and then flees for his life. Only through cleverness and courage does he escape at all. A few days later, he returns with reinforcements from another of Vogel's camps. With firmness tempered with judgment, he puts down the revolt, symbolically blasting to fragments the offending "jimmyjohn," as the cowboy gang's leader mispronounces it. Vogel arrives only in time to pass a benediction on his protégé's victory: "He have joodgement."[11] It is an essential virtue for a Wister hero, and the gaining of it is the subject of many of the author's stories.

Initiation of a different but equally harrowing sort is the subject of "The Promised Land," a story generally ignored by Wister critics. The setting is the wild Okenagon country of Oregon, and the protagonists a family of emigrants from the East who fall under the dubious protection of Wild Goose Jake. He is an apparently benevolent wilderness trader, soon revealed as the territory's most notorious whiskey smuggler, fueling the depravity of the area's Indians. Jake's trade is even more sordid than the simple profiteering of the crooks in "A Pilgrim on the Gila." The emigrants, the Clallam family, meet Jake's half-witted son, who adds a true mean streak to the degeneracy of retardation, perhaps because of Jake's constant abuse. In a series of bestial scenes brought on by Jake's liquor, the drunken Indians nearly kill the family. Jake, however, defends the Clallams, and in a squalid shoot-out, he, his son, and the Indians are all shot. It is an ugly tableau: "Whiskey and blood dripped together, and no one was moving there. It was liquor with some, and death with others, and all of it lay upon the guilty soul of Jake."[12] The story ends as one of Wister's most vivid and uncompromising pictures of the seamy underside of frontier life.

Indian depravity figures also in "A Kinsman of Red Cloud," a story that pits Jarvis Cutler, civilian wagon master for the army, against Toussaint, a wily half-breed card shark and murderer who happens to be related to a Crow chief, Red Cloud. Cutler and some friends trap Toussaint cheating early in the story, and the resulting gunfight leaves Cutler's friends dead and Toussaint an outlaw stalking Cutler for vengeance. The wagon master takes his problem to two friendly lieutenants. One suggests simply killing Toussaint. "How about the commanding officer?" asks the other. "He'd back us—but we'll tell him afterwards" is the reply.[13] When the three go to the Indian agency store to get rifles, they confront the storekeeper: " 'We're going to kill a man,' they explained, and the owner was entirely satisfied." Toussaint is tracked like an animal, shot, and taken into custody. Chief Red Cloud comes dramatically to the fort, demanding to see his kinsman. He stands over the bed of the wounded murderer: "Then the mongrel strain of blood told, and the half-breed poured out a chattering appeal." Red Cloud looks impassively down and then speaks: "Red Cloud says Toussaint heap no good. No Injun, anyhow." Exit the noble full-blooded savage.

"Hank's Woman" similarly treated sordid doings, this time among whites. Wister's first complete story, it suffers from structural awkwardness that Wister intensified in the 1900 version by making one of the characters the Virginian. The central figures are a ne'er-do-well cowboy, Hank, and his mail-order bride, an Austrian peasant, Wilomene. Hank is mean-spirited, shiftless, and suspicious of the strange ways of his docile but stubborn wife, who is firmly rooted in the traditional values of her peasant culture, particularly her religion. Hank abuses her, enraged at her incessant praying which he senses is both a refuge for her and a reproach. One day in a blind rage, he shoots her crucifix, and she cracks and buries an ax in his skull. Driven mad, she flees into the mountains, dragging his body with her, and falls to her death. The story is told by two cowboys whose dialogue forms a superfluous framing action. In the revised version for collection in *The Jimmyjohn Boss,* one of the cowboys is the Virginian, and he passes a Wisterian judgment on the tragic conflict between the Austrian's religion and Hank's trashy lack of values. When the other cowboy comments, "All this fuss just because a woman believed in God," he replies, "You have put it down wrong, it's just because a man didn't."

In the middle of *The Jimmyjohn Boss* are three comic stories— "Sharon's Choice," "Napoleon Shave-Tail," and "Twenty Minutes for Refreshments." None of them is terribly funny—perhaps whimsical is a better word—but all exhibit Wister's shrewd observation and wryly understated reporting of the grotesque and absurd in the West. "Napoleon Shave-Tail" is the least broadly comic of the three. The shave-tail is an insufferable young lieutenant sent to an isolated cavalry fort. An affected martinet, he constantly speaks of the "modernity" of German military methods, alienates the officers and their wives, and is nicknamed "Baby Bismarck" by the men. His bungling of a simple capture of a renegade, however, results in the death of a genial sergeant, and "Napoleon Shave-Tail" is properly humble thereafter. The violence of the sergeant's and the renegade's deaths strike a strange balance with the witty sketches of the long-suffering officers' wives enduring the lieutenant's pomposity, and structurally the story is one of Wister's weakest.

There are no serious overtones to "Sharon's Choice"; there are few overtones of any kind. Sharon is a declining railroad town in the Southwest preparing for its annual elocution contest, the height and extent of the community's efforts at cultural enrichment. The favorites are a young girl, Leola, backed by the women of the town, and a boy, favored by the men, who reads "Baker's Blue Jay Yarn," by Twain. Tempers flare, and it is obvious that the selection of either will enrage half the town. The problem is resolved by unanimous agreement to award the prize to a crippled orphan boy whose halting but courageous delivery of "I love little pussy, her coat is so warm" touches even the hardest hearts.

"Sharon's Choice" is typical of Wister's "cute little shaver" motif, a strong strain in southwestern Local Color fiction, featuring superficially tough characters "fessing up" to the adorableness of babes, urchins, foundlings, and the like. (The epitome of the genre is Harte's "The Luck of Roaring Camp.") Wister shows less finesse than Harte in painting both his children and their admirers. As with the story of the psychotic chicken Em'ly in *The Virginian*, "Sharon's Choice" is cutesy rather than cute. It does, though, have a nicely turned sketch of a young Victorian girl's "repetwar" that Twain might have produced; the girl's sister Arvasita advertises Leola: "Sleep-walking scene, Macbeth . . . Leola's great night at the church fair and bazar [*sic*], El Paso, in Shakespeare's acknowledged masterpiece. Leola's repetwar likewise includes 'Catherine the Queen before her Judges,' 'Quality of Mercy is not Strained,' 'Death of Little Nell,' 'Death of Paul Dombey,' 'Death of the Old Year,' 'Burial of Sir John Moore,' and other standard gems suitable for ladies."[14] The ghost of Emmeline Grangerford hovers over Leola's shoulder.

"Twenty Minutes for Refreshments" is a companion piece to "Sharon's Choice" and a considerable improvement. Another of Wister's neophyte narrators is dragged off a train in the middle of New Mexico by some rough-hewn but gold-hearted locals who want him to judge a baby contest. With him is a vigorous grande dame he has just met, Mrs. Porcher Brewton of Bee Bayou, Louisiana, who has spent the years since "the death of the colonel" traveling western trains and becoming a character in desolate places. It isn't clear whether Wister, and the narrator, regard Mrs. Brewton as a bit too obstreperous in her rubbing elbows with the common people to be *really* well bred, or whether she is meant for eccentric gentry (looking ahead to *real* gentry in *Lady Baltimore,* we suspect the former). The town is in an uproar over the baby contest, orchestrated and manipulated by a salesman pushing Manna Baby Food, who gives Wister a few licks at the drummer personality. The narrator distributes prizes diplomatically enough to placate hot parental hearts, and Mrs. Brewton exerts strong civilizing pressure on a drunken father, Shotgun Smith, determined to seize a prize for his twin babies. The story's strength is in the keenness of Wister's picture of the social interplay of the frontier. As the narrator comments a tad melodramatically at the close, "Oh, George Washington, father of your country, what a brindled litter you have sired!"

The last story of *The Jimmyjohn Boss,* "Padre Ignazio," was a departure for Wister in a number of ways and the best story in the collection. It is about a Spanish priest in San Diego in 1855, and there is not a cowboy about. Most of the dramatic action is in the mind of Padre Ignazio, a cultured man in a cultural desert torn between his desire to end his life among civilized men and the sense of mission that originally sent him on his errand into the wilderness. His temptation is intensified when an educated young traveler, Gaston Villeré, visits the mission. He and the padre spend long hours talking, comparing their lives. Starved for intellectual food, the priest devours Villeré's talk of European culture, particularly the latest opera and other arts. After Villeré goes, Padre Ignazio resolves to leave, but just as he is about to embark for Europe, a gift of gold arrives from Villeré. The young man has made his pile in the goldfields and, mortally wounded in a brawl, has left his money to the priest to buy an organ for the mission. Padre Ignazio takes this gift as a sign from God that he is to resign himself to his lonely calling.

"Padre Ignazio" is an important story in the Wister canon. It was the first major writing after the author's marriage and the last before he plunged into *The Virginian.* Its depth of characterization and consistency of development set it apart from many of the Western tales that rely on slick caricature and deus ex machina twists of plot. Wister is careful to paint the richness of civilized culture as a real and powerful alternative to the priest's faith, so the struggle within him is believable. Further, in exploring the "pre-Saxon" West and creating a sympathetic, thoroughly developed character who is neither American nor culturally and racially Germanic, Wister added breadth to his total Western portrait, counterbalancing its often xenophobic quality.

The Early Stories: Main Themes

Taken as a whole, the fiction in these collections is uneven, and some of it embarrassingly awkward. Still, individual stories are excellent, and many show repeated flashes of the descriptive insight that makes Wister a craftsman comparable to Harte, Bierce, Cable, Garland, O'Hearn, and many more widely heralded journeymen short story writers of the late nineteenth century.

Wister was a vivid writer, but not an extremely inventive one, and therefore these stories exhibit recurrent characters, themes, and techniques. His great theme, of course, was the West itself, and if these tales have enduring value, it must primarily be for their evocation of the land and the culture of the area during the generation from the end of the Civil War to the closing of the frontier; every story in these two collections except "Padre Ignazio" deals with this time. It was a brief period, but also one of those times, like the beginning of the revolution in France or the Athenian Golden Age, that has captured our historical imagination and become disproportionately important in molding a culture's image, both in its own mind and in the world's. It was, as Wister's title for the later book proclaimed, "When West Was West": "Bliss was it in that dawn to be alive."

These stories bristle with this westernism. They are not simply eastern stories of manners and action in a western setting. The action of Crane's "The Blue Hotel" could have been set in Michigan (as Hemingway did in his version, "The Killers"), but "A Pilgrim on the Gila" is aggressively a portrait of a society "somewhere west of Laramie" and east of the Sierras.

Underlying the action of these stories, or rather overshadowing it, is the enormous presence of the physical land itself, with that intense sense of space that Charles Olsen said was central to all true American fiction.[15] Wister was to do even better with landscape in *The Virginian,* in which he polished to perfection the sense of isolation and exhilaration of the individual drawn against an immensity of land and sky. The early stories, however, also present again and again the immediacy of the physical scene and its ability to overwhelm with beauty or blight. Wister's writing can be moving: "The sun came up, and with a stroke struck the world to crystal. The near sand-hills went into rose, and the crabbed yucca and the mesquite turned transparent, with lances and pale films of green, like drapery graciously veiling the desert's face, and distant violet peaks and edges framed the vast enchantment beneath the liquid exhalations of the sky."[16]

Alternately invigorating in its beauty or depressing and threatening in its desolation, Wister's Janus-faced nature is appropriate to the duality of his attitude toward a western world that was appealing for its freedom and disturbing for its lack of control. Often the natural world of these stories is one of peace and purity in contrast to the sordid reality of society and the pressures of adjusting to the corrupt world. The two cowboys in "Hank's Woman" fish and swim in an idyllic mountain pool while they struggle to understand a seamy story of life in town; the hero of "The Jimmyjohn Boss" flees the brutality of the line camp to find refuge in the solemn beauty of a winter night; and Specimen Jones in his pre-army days is a wanderer largely because he finds the wilderness cleaner than the ways of men. Just as often, though, nature is a stern taskmaster and an exhausting opponent. Two of Wister's bleakest pictures are of the struggles of the troops on a winter march in "The General's Bluff" and the emigrant family of "The Promised Land" fighting a constant battle against a blasted desert land of twisted rock and raging rivers. Nowhere is nature more inimical than in "La Tinaja Bonita," in which it assumes the implacable, almost predatory character it has in deterministic naturalist fiction such as the closing scene of Frank Norris's *McTeague*.

However effectively presented, the world of nature is only a backdrop for Wister's central concern, the delineation of frontier society. True to his breeding, Wister was always an observer of manners, good or bad. The most fascinating thing about the West to him was that it was a land of new social nuances, a place where he had to learn anew what "the right sort of people" were supposed to do. He is perhaps less concerned in this early writing with establishing a sense of nostalgia than in his later work, and neither has he solidified his vision of the West as a battleground between good and evil, the great themes that were to inform his Western writing after 1900. Already, though, the moral imperatives of the later fiction are becoming apparent.

As with *The Virginian,* the world of these stories is one in which the forces of barbarism are frequently locked in combat with the forces of civilization and decent behavior. The balance is a tenuous one. In a number of stories, good men—or the good in men—succumb to a world of bestial impulses. "Salvation Gap," "La Tinaja

Bonita," "A Pilgrim on the Gila," "The Promised Land," and
"Hank's Woman" are grim studies in which man's worst instincts—
treachery, greed, jealousy, envy—are given free rein, uncontrolled or
only partly checked by decency, reason, and respect for order.

It is a concern for order that is central to Wister's moral vision in
Red Men and White and *The Jimmyjohn Boss*. With the possible excep-
tions of the three comic stories in *The Jimmyjohn Boss* and "Padre Ignazio," there isn't a Wister story of the 1890s in which the central
conflict is not between representatives of authority and order and the
forces of anarchy. The redoubtable army checks the savages in the Indian stories, God-fearing emigrants oppose brutal libertarians in
"Hank's Woman" and "The Promised Land," and in "A Pilgrim on
the Gila" and "The Second Missouri Compromise", the forces of effective government struggle with promoters of lawlessness, losing in
the first case, prevailing in the second.

Almost invariably, Wister's voice of authority is somehow duly
constituted. Not only do men like Dean Drake, General Crook, and
Governor Ballard project a sense of moral gravity, but they also carry
some kind of portfolio: trail boss, military leader, elected official.
Even in "Padre Ignazio," a story that is in many ways sui generis,
the central figure is an ordained priest whose religious office is the
only institutional authority in an untamed and barbarous land. Only
Specimen Jones defies the pattern in the story "Specimen Jones," in
which he is an itinerant miner, although a father figure to young
Cumnor. Perhaps Wister felt uncomfortable that Jones lacked offi-
cially delegated authority, because he immediately put him in uni-
form in "The General's Bluff" and promoted him to sergeant in "The
Second Missouri Compromise."

Two characteristics distinguish the responsible leaders of Wister's
rough western society, competence and judgment, and although the
two usually go hand in hand, they are not necessarily concurrent.
Competence is the scrupulous attention to detail and profound
knowledge of terrain of General Crook, Dean Drake's ability with a
gun, Specimen Jones's "talent for killing Indians" which Crook
prizes, and Cutler's skill with horses in "A Kinsman of Red Cloud."
Judgment concerns leadership, management of men, and the ability
to interpret and understand western life beyond simply functioning
effectively. It is "joodgement" that Max Vogel sends Drake to the
dangerous trail camp to learn, judgment that Jones shows extricating
Governor Ballard from his sticky confrontation with ex-Confederates

who are not yet ex-rebels, and judgment that makes Padre Ignazio renounce his impulse to abandon his calling.

In whatever form they appear, the authoritarians have Wister's unqualified approval. Often he waxes eloquent on the wonderfulness of authority, as in his description of an army outpost in "A Pilgrim on the Gila": "Here were lieutenants, captains, a major, and a colonel, American citizens with a love of their country and a standard of honor. . . . The day was punctuated with the bright trumpet, people went and came in the simple dignity of duty, and once again I talked with good men and women. God bless our soldier people: I said it often."[17]

He says it very often, but not perhaps as frequently as he damns the contrasting riffraff who threaten constantly to overturn order and cast society into a seamy chaos. Rootless and shiftless, the common man threatens the social structure with anarchy in every story. Even at his best, when he lacks malevolence as well as discipline, Wister's proletarian is a willful child, as with the cowboys of "The Jimmyjohn Boss": "The children, the primitive, pagan, dangerous children."[18] Although exhilarating in their spontaneity and bursting with admirable energy, they are ominously lacking in the moral and spiritual depth that would restrain their scarcely latent animalism: "The body was all that the buccaroos knew; well, the flesh comes pretty natural to all of us—and who ever taught these men about the spirit?"[19] These same careless, reckless cowboys form much of the cast of *Lin McLean* and *The Virginian;* the first traces Lin's progress out of their amoral limbo, the second consistently asserts the Virginian's responsible superiority to it.

At his worst, the irresponsible common man of these stories becomes the blood-lusting lynch mob, the corrupt jury ready to sell justice for a handful of silver, or the primitive Indians howling for white scalps. Even in comic stories like "Twenty Minutes for Refreshments," there is the constant threat that the kind of people who name their children out of romantic novels will revert to rapacious basic instincts if social procedure doesn't please them: when a man is about to resort to violence if his children lose a beauty contest, Mrs. Porcher Brewton as the voice of authority must remind him, "You are going to behave yourself like the gentleman you are, and not the wild beast that's inside you."[20]

Wister's stories of the 1890s do not show as strongly the racial biases evident in *The Virginian* and blatant in *Lady Baltimore* (1906),

but already Wister was identifying the forces of disorder and brutish-
ness with "lesser" races and classes. Inevitably, characters not of pure
Anglo-Saxon blood come off as worthless or worse. The young,
deadly Mexico gigolo of "La Tinaja Bonita" is "a spruce, pretty boy,
not likely to toil severely";[21] Wister contrasts his face to that of the
American Genesmere and his "bronzed Saxon face, almost as young
as his own, but of sterner stuff . . . powerful, blue-eyed, his mus-
tache golden, his cheek clean-cut, and beaten into shining health by
the weather."[22] Mormons are several times called "thieving," and the
chief crook of "A Pilgrim on the Gila" is a Mormon elder.

For Indians Wister has a bit more sympathy, although he clearly
sees them as inferior to his Saxon heroes. Still, as long as they stay to
themselves and accept the governance of the white man with his superior powers of reason, they maintain a certain simplistic nobility,
and Wister now and then admits that they have gotten a raw deal.
General Crook, for example, is both the epitome of the Indian-fight-
ing general and an apologist for the red men who can no longer hunt
freely as their fathers could. Wister's attitude toward the Indian is
similar to that of the paternalistic southern apologists toward the Negro, and like the southerners, Wister claimed an understanding of
the primitive mind and an appreciation of it. Of a young and bigoted
cavalry officer new to the West, Wixter comments, "He held the reg-
ulation Eastern view that the Indian knows nothing but the three
blind appetites."[23] Wister gives him credit for more, but it is a back-
handed compliment: "So far from being a mere animal, the Indian is
of a subtlety more ancient than the Sphinx. In his primal brain—
nearer nature than our own—the directness of a child mingles with
the profoundest cunning. He believes easily in powers of light and
darkness, yet is a sceptic all the while."[24]

For the pure-blooded Indian Wister has respect, but the half-breed
is a mongrel abomination. Throughout Wister's work runs an ugly
condemnation of miscegenation, and it is full-blown in the early stories. Toussaint, the villain of "A Kinsman of Red Cloud," is a product of "a French trapper from Canada out of a Sioux squaw, one of
Red Cloud's sisters, and his heart beat hot with the evil of two races,
and none of their good."[25] *Mongrel* and *half-breed* are two of Wister's
favorite pejorative terms, and at times he uses them simply metaphorically, as when Dean Drake calls the motley gang of cowboys he
must tame "a half-breed lot."

Wister's society in these collections is polarized by these two groups—the upright, competent upholders of law and order and the irresponsible, valueless trash who are either actually lawless or simply amoral. Wister was too good a writer, though, to break his world down into only "white hats" and "black hats," and many of his characters are neither. The comic stories "Sharon's Choice," "Twenty Minutes for Refreshments," and "Napoleon Shave-Tail," for example, have characters who are simply whimsical eccentrics. Specimen Jones and Cutler of "A Kinsman of Red Cloud" are decent and competent men, but high spirits and wanderlust keep both of them from falling into the good gray foreman image of the Virginian. Wister also granted what he doubtless felt was a gentlemanly latitude toward his women, for they can display irresponsibility, and it only makes them flighty rather than damned. The flirtations of the Mexican girl Lolita in "La Tinaja Bonita" are attributable to a passionate nature. The silly women of Siskiyou whose sympathy for cold-blood murderers provokes a lynching are presented as lacking judgment rather than morality, and once the hanging is over and they have been properly rebuked, they are forgiven. Women have not become, however, in these stories, the civilizing force that Wister makes of them in *The Virginian,* and Howells was voicing the consensus of critical reaction when he wrote of *Red Men and White* that it was "a man's book throughout."[26]

Wister's vision in these stories of a frontier balanced between order and anarchy included an attitude toward justice frequently disparaged by Wister's critics and disturbing, we know, even to his family and friends.[27] Although not exactly a promoter of lynch law, Wister was at times an apologist, and his feelings about vigilante justice were ambivalent at best. The lynch story has a considerable history in American literature—Dreiser's "Nigger Jeff," Faulkner's "Dry September," and Baldwin's "Going to Meet the Man" are only three distinguished examples. It is a recurrent theme in Wister. Actually, his handling of the subject in one story, "Salvation Gap," is much like that of Dreiser, Faulkner, and Baldwin. The story is brutal, direct, and vivid, and the reader has a sense of the action being driven by human and natural forces out of control and grimly deterministic. There is no doubt in "Salvation Gap" that the mob that lynches the wrong man is an ugly thing, and both the sympathetic sheriff who pleads for law and compassion and the stolid, guilt-ridden killer make the story unequivocally one of justice gone wrong.

In other stories, though, rough justice receives a much better press. In "Little Bighorn Medicine," Wister repeatedly complains that the soldiers are unable to "discipline" the potentially insurgent Indians—meaning shoot them—because it might touch off a court of inquiry. Cutler and his army friends do not feel so handicapped in "A Kinsman of Red Cloud," and it's only by accident that they don't kill Toussaint in cold blood, although they shoot him when he's unarmed. Wister's most disturbing, and most casual, attitude toward vigilante action surfaces in the climax of "The Serenade at Siskiyou" in which the pillars of the community string up a couple of stage robbers apparently only to teach the feckless womenfolk a lesson.

Even in stories in which there is not an actual lynching or murder in the name of justice, the threat is just under the surface. In "La Tinaja Bonita," the hero Genesmere three times decides to kill the boy Luis before the Mexican has a chance to kill him; in "The General's Bluff," the army debates making a preemptive strike against the Indians; and in "A Pilgrim on the Gila," the narrator decides that lynching might be the only way to ensure justice in the teeth of a rigged jury. Perhaps the most perverse example of vigilantism occurs in "The Promised Land," in which the degenerate whiskey smuggler, Wild Goose Jake, shoots up a roomful of Indians whom he has besotted with drink, because they *might* hurt someone. Jake believes the killings, which he feels are in defense of the emigrant family that has stumbled into his squalid den, are a noble act of protecting the righteous.

It is perhaps unfair in dealing with *Red Men and White* and *The Jimmyjohn Boss* to emphasize too greatly Wister's presentation of frontier justice. Unquestionably he was an unabashed authoritarian, and he often seems to be apologizing for the sudden "judicial" violence of the West, a "justice" that sometimes borders on the lawlessness he detested. Still, these early stories in particular present a rough and brutal world, and Wister persistently points out that the West is *different* and that coming to know it truly is to realize that the rules of eastern life do not apply. If Wister's heroes are quick on the trigger or with a rope, it is in response to an environment that is genuinely dangerous and in which the forces of lawlessness and chaos consistently threaten. Certainly, sometimes Wister seems to be not only describing the psychology of lynch law, but approving it. Still, we must remember that the world of that psychology was his *donée*. We can hardly criticize him because the mechanics of justice in Wyoming were not as deliberate as those of Dickens's Chancery. In some ways, as Wister and Dickens both indicate, they were less ugly.

Whatever their weaknesses in terms of authoritarianism and racism, these early Western stories established Wister's image of the West and went a long way toward printing it indelibly upon the American consciousness. Nearly all the elements of Wister's later Western writing are here: the vivid, realistic description of a strange, wild physical world; careful observation and delineation of strange and often comic social machinery; rich characterization in the best tradition of the Local Color school; a flair for the vignette and a narrative gift for catching the ironic twists of life that make stories out of simple accounts; an unflinching realism, almost a Naturalist determination not to romanticize the quality of western life, even when dramatizing its action; and two thematic concerns—first, to present the West as genuinely unique, distinct from anything familiar to the reader, and second, to present that world as a field upon which the old forces of order and disorder, quality and trash, moral strength and moral weakness, good and bad, contended as they always have in Wister's vision, in all worlds, old or new.

Finally, the early fiction is a crucial basis for that to come. In *The Virginian,* Wister would set a hero in this spontaneous new world. In his later Western fiction, he would shift his emphasis from celebrating its presence to mourning its passing.

Chapter Four

Lin McLean

Plots in All Directions

Like most of Wister's published works, his first attempt at a novel, *Lin McLean,* was an uncommonly long time in production. *Red Men and White* was published in November of 1895, and Wister was then working on the stories that would make up *Lin McLean.* Much of the second book had actually already been written. "How Lin McLean Went East" had appeared in print as early as 1892, followed by "The Winning of the Biscuit-Shooter" (1893), "Lin McLean's Honeymoon" (1894), and "A Journey in Search of Christmas" (1895). "The Burial of the Biscuit-Shooter," which Wister retitled "Destiny at Drybone" and revised slightly for its inclusion in the novel, was written in 1895, but not published until December of 1897 simultaneously with the total novel (the date on the copyright page is 1898). *Lin McLean* was therefore written over a span of five years, and somewhat rewritten, edited, and pulled together in the first half of 1897.[1]

Wister was evidently well aware of the book's structural limitations at the time of publication. Instead of dividing the novel into chapters, as was even more the custom in the 1890s than it is today, he split it into "episodes," each a long short story. Ten years later, after the success of *The Virginian* made a second edition of the earlier book profitable, Wister broke *Lin McLean* into shorter, more conventional chapters which tend to disguise the great narrative gaps between the "episodes" of the earlier printing. For this second edition, Wister wrote a somewhat defensive preface which both acknowledged and denied the book's lack of thematic integrity. It is worth quoting at length, for it provides insight into his attitudes toward fiction and also foreshadows a long, rancorous war of words between Wister and other literary men over "declining standards" in American literature, a debate that would become a cause célèbre during and after World War I:

Through my forgetting that appearances generally count for more than real-
ities, *Lin McLean* has always ranked as a collection of short stories, whereas,
after the young hero's first adventure with his elder brother and the bishop,
a plot begins with the entrance of the "biscuit-shooter," and steadily proceeds through climax and catastrophe to solution. After some fifteen years
there is no harm in disclosing my scheme of construction—something not
well for the author to do while engaged on his work. It was my aim to tell
a long story, not through a series of chapters in the usual way, but through
a chain of short stories, each not only a complete adventure in itself, but
also a fragment of an under-lying drama. Thus each new link inherited from
its predecessor a situation which it developed and passed on to its successor.
I had hoped that this somewhat unusual device might be noticed, and possibly create a little interest; but I had overlooked the fact that matters of
craftsmanship do not fall into the light of critical attention here as they do
in Europe, where the writer is held as much accountable for his manner of
saying a thing as for the thing he says.[2]

In defending his "novel," Wister was deluded if he thought the book
was a triumph of subtle interlocking of plot elements, for structure
and transition are surely the work's greatest weaknesses; its plots ride
off in all directions.

For all its lack of focus, though, the basic action of *Lin McLean* is
not complicated. The first three chapters introduce the hero, a footloose, fun-loving cowboy of nineteen, long on decency but short on
responsibility. We first see him in central Wyoming and follow him
around the West for two or three years, a journey of literally thousands of miles, while he loses his money at cards, courts a servant
girl, digs for gold, and, of all things, serves ice cream in an Arizona·
drugstore. All the while, Lin vows that he's going to return to his
childhood home in Boston for a visit, and at the end of the first "episode" he does so. Tanned and dressed for the trail, Lin cuts a strange
figure in the East. His older brother, last of the family, is a parvenue
dry-goods clerk who snubs Lin the moment the cowboy arrives and
is ashamed to be seen in public with him. After telling the brother
off, Lin wanders desolately around his childhood haunts, feeling increasingly out of place, and then catches a train west. Not until he
gets back to the wide open spaces does he feel comfortable, and he
realizes that the West is his home.

The next four chapters (in the 1907 edition) involve Lin's luckless
and obtuse courting of a blowzy, brash ex-waitress whom everybody

but Lin calls "the biscuit-shooter" (a girl who hustles food for railroad crews in track-side eateries). Although fifteen years Lin's senior, the biscuit-shooter stirs his hormones, and he woos her, competing with a seedy sagebrush Romeo named Tommy who runs the local stage stop and is regarded by the cowboys as a "sad bird." Only Lin and Tommy are too dense to realize that the girl is trash, attested to for the reader by such unimpeachable authority as the Bishop of Wyoming, who keeps popping up as the voice of authority in Wister's writing, and the Virginian himself, whom Wister was warming up for his own novel and whose elegant courtship of Molly Wood, developed in *The Virginian,* is contrasted here to Lin's tawdry affair. Lin is unfortunate enough to win the biscuit-shooter's indelicate hand, they marry in a hasty and undignified ceremony, and for a few weeks she makes his life miserable, abusing him in public and private and firmly curtailing the casual freedom that was Lin's joy. At this time, however, a rainmaker comes to parched Cheyenne, the scene of this part of the novel. His assistant is another "pretty poor bird" named Lusk, whom the governor suddenly recognizes as the biscuit-shooter's ex-husband, abandoned but still legally married to her. There is a predictable comic confrontation at the same time that the rainmaker's fulminations actually produce rain: the biscuit-shooter chooses Lusk and leaves with him, and Lin is a free man, not much sadder, but wiser.

Wister obviously felt that his next episode was a logical development of the biscuit-shooter courtship, but only through unconvincing contrivance does he make it so. The novel shifts abruptly some years ahead to a Christmas, presumably in the late 1880s. Lin drifts into Cheyenne at loose ends, looking for a good time. He tags along with his old friend the governor, who is buying gifts, and Lin realizes how full is the life of a man of responsibility and how empty is his own. Belligerently, he takes a train to Denver, resolved to spend Christmas there in an orgy of expensive food, drink, and—Wister discreetly implies—women. Arriving on Christmas Eve, he is suddenly beset by three street urchins competing to shine his boots. Gruff but gentle, Lin banters with them and wins their trust. The orgy is forgotten, and he spends the evening treating the waifs to dinner and a vaudeville show. He is shocked to discover that the littlest and most winsome of the boys is Billy, the runaway son of Lusk and the biscuit-shooter, neither of whom Lin has seen in the intervening years. Lin takes Billy back to Wyoming with him and "sort of adopts" him.

It's obvious, though, that the boy needs a "real home," and this leads Wister to his final episode, the coming of the "true girl," Jessamine Buckner. Like Lin, she is appropriately weak on education and formal breeding, but full of decency and grit. She has come to Wyoming from Kentucky to get her shiftless, braggart brother pardoned by the ubiquitous governor, and she succeeds. She spends a night among the riotous but good-natured cowboys at a rail stop, sleeping in a boxcar watched over by the instantly smitten Lin. Jessamine retrieves her brother, who manages, in an unconvincing scene, to get killed by a horse. She is crushed, but stays on in Wyoming, at first repulsing Lin's attempts to console her. Soon, though, she gets a job tending the railroad station, she and little Billy take to each other, and it seems the inevitable betrothal is just around the corner.

The course of true love, in Wister, never does run smooth. Jessamine finds out about Lin's brief, illegal marriage, and she tells him that, although she will marry no one else, she cannot marry him because he has "a wife livin'." Her logic is murky, but she sticks to her guns and exiles Lin with Billy to a ranch he's been preparing for her in the mountains. For months they live unhappily apart, until one day Lusk and the biscuit-shooter arrive without warning to bring the novel to its conclusion. The biscuit-shooter has not mellowed, but she has evidently picked up some compassion. She visits first Jessamine and then Lin, trying to persuade each that they are made for each other and that Lin never loved her. Then, in a chaotic climax, she poisons herself dramatically in the middle of a barroom dance. It isn't clear whether she does this to free Lin or in remorse at her ill-spent life. Lin and the governor, who is also a doctor, try to save her in vain, and Wister provides a genuinely moving account of her funeral. Jessamine, Lin, and little Billy live happily ever after.

Structure, Style, and Characterization

The novel is not nearly as fatuous as a paraphrase of it makes it appear, although there are sections in which the sentimentality becomes positively painful, notably the coy scenes between Lin and the street urchins. Jessamine Buckner is "as stiff as a board," as Frederic

Remington, who did the illustrations, put it.[3] There are substantial difficulties in overall structure. The opening section detailing Lin's wanderings and recognition of his westernism is too radically detached from the episode on the coming of the biscuit-shooter. Lin's Christmas encounter with the urchins is a separate entity, and it is only through the long and unconvincing arm of Dickensian coincidence that the one he fastens on turns out to be his sometime-wife's child. Until Jessamine finds out about Lin's marriage, the section on the "true girl" in no way proceeds out of the previous biscuit-shooter action. When Jessamine rejects Lin, we feel that her motives are obscure and contrived, which is Wister's effort to twist the plot back into an earlier channel.

The worst structural problems lie in awkwardness of development and transition within the separate episodes. This is the same difficulty with pacing exhibited throughout Wister's fiction. Like a faulty movie projector, Wister allows action to move at a snail's pace and then abruptly snaps the reader forward, leaving the disquieting impression of jerkiness. Thus, after lengthy development, the section on Lin's rescue of young Billy peters out completely: Lin wonders in one paragraph in Denver whatever he is to do with the boy and half a page later decides he'll find him a place on a ranch—or something ("why, I'll fix it somehow"). The death of Jessamine's brother is another example: Wister builds him up extensively as a threatening character and an obstacle to Lin's courtship and then suddenly disposes of him through an accident.

Analagous to the problem of shifting pace is that of the shifting narrator. The introductory section on "How Lin McLean Went East," the account of Lin's Christmas, and the closing section on the death of the biscuit-shooter are presented in omniscient third person. Interposed, however, are the episodes on the courtship of the biscuit-shooter and the coming of Jessamine, which use a first-person narrative persona who injects himself into the story to carry on extensive dialogue with the main characters and to remind us persistently of his raconteur presence: "Perhaps I should have told you before that Separ was a place once—a sort of place; but you will relish now, I am convinced, the pithy fable of its name" (169). We might relish it more if it were presented to us without chatty comment.

The narrator often produces this cloying, intrusive "gentle reader" style, reminiscent of Hawthorne's "damned mob of scribbling women," and it is a style that characterizes too much of the novel.

Lin McLean ends with a poem that concludes: "Far 'neath the huge invading dusk / Comes Silence awful through the plain; / But yonder horseman's heart is gay, / And he goes singing might and main" (303). The novel sometimes outpontificates Longfellow on the long, long thoughts of youth: "Who knows the child-soul, young in days, yet old as Adam and the hills?" (198).

Irritating as this style is, Wister atones for it with some direct descriptive writing and some neatly turned dialogue that is as good as anything in his fiction and compares favorably with the best of nineteenth-century prose. Characteristically, Wister is at his best as an understated and objective observer or reporter of the natural scene. His picture of the face of the land—the plains and mountains, the camps and towns—set a high standard for Western literature to follow. His physical description is comparable to the best of Parkman and superior to all of Irving's *Tour on the Prairies* (1835). Like a verbal Remington, Wister catches scenes and moments and freezes them, letting images speak for themselves. *Lin McLean* is full of such scenes. A typical one is the account of the biscuit-shooter's funeral, at which a random assembly of hung-over cowboys sing "Streets of Laredo": "When the song was ended, they left the graveyard quietly and went down the hill. The morning was growing warm. Their work waited them across many sunny miles of range and plain. Soon their voices and themselves had emptied away into the splendid vastness and silence, and they were gone. . . . In Drybone's deserted quadrangle the sun shone down upon Lusk still sleeping, and the wind shook the aces and kings in the grass" (300). Graceful understatement is characteristic of the best of Wister's early style, and there is much of it in *Lin McLean*. The vivid vignettes, casually set out and not overstressed, mark the most colorful, and the most pictorial, sections. Speaking of one of Lin's friends, Honey Wiggin, and a brush with violence, Wister writes: "Through excellent card-playing he won a pinto from a small Mexican horse-thief who came into the town from the South and who cried bitterly when he delivered up his pet pony to the new owner. The new owner, being a man of the world and agile on his feet, was only slightly stabbed that evening as he walked to the dance-hall at the edge of town. The Mexican was buried on the next day but one" (29).

Dialogue in the novel is as erratic as the descriptive prose. Some sections move quickly and believably. Much of the clipped, direct banter is superior to some of the pompous philosophizing and folksy cuteness of much of *The Virginian*. In other sections, though, Wister lets his characters slip into a queer, circuitous rambling that obscures the subject, somewhat like the roundabout "Ratliff" style of some of Faulkner's narratives, but far less appropriate. Thus, the biscuit-shooter to Jessamine on the nature of love: "Do you know that you have hurt a good man's heart? For once I hurt it myself, though different. And hurts in them kind of hearts stays. Some hearts is that luscious and pasty you can stab 'em and it closes up so yu'd never suspicion the place—but Lin McLean? Nor yet don't yus believe his is the kind that breaks—if any kind does that. You may sit till the gray hairs, and you may wall up your womanhood, but if a man has got manhood like him, he will never sit till the gray hairs" (256).

If consistency of structure and style troubled Wister, characterization did not. At the center of the novel, Lin is a fully delineated and believable figure, if a bit lacking in depth. His development is consistent. He opens as a careless child, "gay," to use Wister's word, who embodies the spontaneous spirit of the West. He is goodhearted, but callow and totally without focus, a kind of pixie of the plains, drifting without malice or ambition through a pastiche of western scenes. Loose women, card games, mining camps, and drinking sprees are interposed with periods of hard work (although we see far more of Lin at play than at work). "Variety, you bet!" is his watchword. At the opening of the novel, he is the composite of the free, decent, but irresponsible cowboy of the early days of the range. His foreman, who calls him "satisfactory . . . good-hearted, willing, a plumb dare-devil with a horse," sketches him plain:

Came in the country about seventy-eight, I believe, and rode for the Bordeaux Outfit most a year and quit. Blew in at Cheyenne till he went broke, and worked over on to the Platte. Rode for the C.Y. Outfit most a year, and quit. Blew in at Buffalo. Rode for Balaam awhile on Butte Creek. Broke his leg. Went to the Drybone Hospital, and when the fracture was commencing to knit pretty good he broke it again at the hog-ranch across the bridge. Next time you're in Cheyenne get Dr. Barker to tell you about that. McLean drifted to Green River last year and went up over on to Snake and up Snake, and was around with a prospecting outfit on Galena Creek by Pitchstone Canyon. Seems he got interested in some Dutchwoman up there, but she had trouble—died, I think they said—and he came down by Meteetsee to Wind River. He's liable to go to Mexico or Africa next. (8)

Lin's slow progression from such casual and riotous rootlessness is the core of the novel. Never quick mentally, Lin's "untrained manly soul" needs a combination of the hard lessons of life and the guiding hands of several mentors and one good woman to lead him to peace and stability, but his gradual and complete acceptance of responsibility parallels that of his society.

The other characters are vivid, although Wister, like many Local Color writers, is often tempted to sacrifice depth and believability to eccentricity. The free-spirited cowboys—Honey Wiggan and the rest—form a predictable supporting chorus for Lin's footloose nature, always ready for a joke or a spree. They are balanced by such voices of wisdom and authority as the Virginian, the governor, and the bishop. Drifting on the periphery are a collection of colorful western oddities: "Jode (Poinsett Middleton Manigault Jode) respresenting five of the oldest families in South Carolina . . . and Long Island" (11) clinging to his Anglican manners and clothes, although "he came to see that Wyoming was a game invented after his book of rules was published"; the rainmaker, who blows into Cheyenne with a truckful of mysterious paraphernalia and a convoluted spiel nobody can understand; Texas, the lovelorn child cowboy who follows Jessamine around like a whipped puppy. Wister is good at thumbnail characterization. Of waitresses at a track stop, he writes that the group was "a platoon of Amazons. . . . It hymned the total bill-of-fare at a blow. In this inexpressible ceremony the name of every dish went hurtling into the next, telescoped to shapelessness. Moreover, if you stopped your Amazon in the middle, it dislocated her, and she merely went back and took a fresh start" (58).

The Western Experience

This is the true strength of *Lin McLean*—the rich portrait of the variety of the western experience in terms both of characters and of the land on which they live. This is not to say, however, that the novel is utterly lacking thematic integrity. Although the cutting and pasting are too obvious, Wister had a conception of the shape and development of the novel he wanted to write. The book is essentially a *bildungsroman* tracing the progress from youth to maturity of a central figure whose development is emblematic of that of the society in which he lives. Lin's raw immaturity is mirrowed throughout the novel by the raw immaturity of the West itself. Even the elusive narrator shares in the learning process. When he first appears, he informs us, "Perhaps manhood was not quite established in my own soul at that time—and perhaps that is the reason why it is the only time I

have ever known which I would live over again, those years when
people said, 'You are old enough to know better'—and one didn't
care!'' (46).

Wister, ever the Philadelphia patrician, makes no bones about the
weaknesses of the cowboy nature, although he does claim its spontaneity rescues it from true malevolence. He sees the cowboys as
healthy animals, lacking in wisdom and needing direction. When the
cowboys at Separ habitually shoot up the railroad's water tank to "ed-
ucate" a station agent, and return an investigating sheriff to the railroad tied to a cowcatcher with the sign "Send us along one dozen as
per sample," the lenient narrator says, "Now what should authority
do upon these free plains, this wilderness of do-as-you-please, where
mere breathing the air was like inebriation? The large, headlong children who swept in from the sage-brush and out again meant nothing
that they called harm until they found themselves resisted . . . [but]
they valued their own lives as little, and that lifts them forever from
baseness at least" (172).

If there is a key word to characterize the "spirit of the West"
which lies at the heart of *Lin McLean,* it is *childlike.* Repeatedly, Wister refers to Lin in just these terms—as a "child of the range," "child
of freedom," "child-man," and a "child at play." Interestingly, the
biscuit-shooter and Jessamine are both repeatedly called "girls," in
juxtaposition to Molly Wood, who in this book and *The Virginian* is
emphatically "the woman." And even though Lin mellows into a
kind of maturity at the end, his naive child nature persists, as the
novel's last sentence indicates: "That cabin on Box Elder became a
home in truth, with a woman inside taking the only care of Mr.
McLean that he had known since his childhood; though singularly
enough he has an impression that it is he who takes care of Jessamine!" (303).

Balancing Lin's Peter Pan nature, and the whole wild *spiritus mundi*
of the cowboy West, are those familiar Wisterian éminences grises,
the representatives of law and order, civilization, culture, and adulthood. The three most prominent are the Virginian, Governor Barker,
and the Bishop of Wyoming, who appear repeatedly in Wister stories
and three or four times each in *Lin McLean* to counterpoint some aspect of Lin's immaturity. The Virginian teases him repeatedly for his
wild, wicked ways, and he is never mentioned without Wister reminding the reader of his dignified courtship of the well-bred and reserved Molly, the epitome of what civilized mating should be. The

governor serves as a paradigm of social behavior for Lin; although still
hard-drinking and able to swear, he has now shouldered civic responsibility. The bishop is the image of maturity of soul who gives Lin a
bit of scripture and an occasional blessing, and reminds him now and
then of the potential comfort of religion. Wister is very careful, by
the way, to stress the strongly masculine nature of each of these civ-
ilizers. The Virginian is always called "big" or "grave," the governor
a "friend of men"; in the case of the bishop, the narrator bends over
backwards. He is a "hearty type . . . familiar with the gear of vehi-
cles," who understands swearing. When asked if the Bishop is a good
man, a tough foreman replies, "He's better than that; he's a man"
(19).

Wister is much concerned for the masculinity of his voices of authority, because in his fiction the process of civilization increasingly
became identified with the feminization of the West and the battle of
the sexes, nowhere more strikingly than in *Lin McLean* and *The Virginian*. We see the taming and ordering influence of the female more
dramatically, perhaps, in the latter novel, but it is still critical in *Lin
McLean,* in which women appear in two masks: as the mindless, sexual, repressive Katy Lusk, and as the calming, nurturing, ordering
figure of Jessamine Buckner. The virago biscuit-shooter embodies
only the role of woman as a threat to masculine freedom. As the narrator says: "I felt a rising hate for the ruby-cheeked, large-eyed eat-
ing-house lady, the biscuit-shooter whose influence was dimming this
jaunty, irrepressible spirit [Lin]. . . . Her bulky bloom had ensnared
him, and now she was going to tame and spoil him" (86). Jessamine,
though, is all honey and crude dignity. Literally from the moment
that Lin sets eyes on her, he dedicates himself toward ordering his
life so as to be worthy of her.

As is the case with the Virginian and Molly Wood, Lin offers no
resistance to Jessamine's intrusion into his free life. Still, as in *The
Virginian* and a number of other Wister stories, a subtle but pitched
battle of the sexes must be played out before the free-spirited cowboy
can be brought to rein. Peculiarly, with Jessamine as with Molly, it
is the woman who is most resistant to the accommodation, in the
tradition of courtly love. After she exiles Lin on the technicality of
having a living wife, Jessamine holds out for months against his entreaties. The narrator says: "I saw that she was weeping and that beneath the tyranny of her resolution her whole loving ample nature
was wrung. But the strange, narrow fibre in her would not yield"

(204). It is as if civilizing women must have proved to them the
worth of the wild western men they would tame and of the crude
western world into which they must be assimilated. It can only be
suggested that Wister himself, notably as a legacy from his hyperrefined mother, perceived civilization as feminine. He may also have
sensed in himself the tension between the "feminine" East and the
"masculine" West. One of his most interesting letters to his mother
discusses how she and her refined friends would hate the West.[4] He
must have felt the resistance of the East and the need of the West to
be "proven" in order to be accepted.

If Lin and Jessamine play out the struggle between feminine re-
straint and masculine freedom as do the Virginian and Molly in *The
Virginian,* Wister does not accentuate the conflict between East and
West as strongly as in the later book. Molly is from an upper-class
family, and she is very much concerned that her refinement will not
mesh with her lover's lack of it. Jessamine, however, is from rural
Kentucky and peasant stock, so, although Lin feels that she is "better" than he, that superiority is not so much cultural and social as
emotional, and it certainly isn't regional. In fact, although the reader
is reminded through *Lin McLean* of the dichotomy between eastern
and western life, the actual dramatic confrontation between the regions is disposed of in the first episode, "How Lin McLean Went
East," when Lin is snubbed by his brother and realizes that his home
is Wyoming, not Boston.

Similarly, if Wister's perception of the distance between East and
West is not as strong in *Lin McLean* as in later writings, neither is
his transference of Wisterian values. The novel is without the long
paragraphs discussing "quality" that weight many chapters of *The
Virginian.* The obvious distinctions between the vulgar biscuit-
shooter and her even trashier husband Lusk and the decency of Lin
and Jessamine are evident, but not belabored. Still, Wister's prejudices surface now and then. Lin, who can hardly read, explains to a
station agent that "Wall Street . . . has been lunched on by them
Ross-childs, and they're moving on. Feeding along to Chicago"
(173). A cowboy thinking to find a room for Jessamine, asks another
about the condition of a railroad section house: "Rank . . . since
those Italians used it. The pump engineer has been scouring but he's
scared to bunk there yet himself" (186). There is consciousness of
caste and class, but not to the extent found in other Wister writing.
For the most part, the social picture in this novel is one of the West

before the Fall, before the social evils of the East descended. Wister puts it just this way when writing of the governor: "Wyoming's Chief Executive knocked elbows with the spurred and jingling waif, one man as good as another in that raw, hopeful, full-blooded cattle era, which now the sobered West remembers as the days of its fond youth. For one man has been as good as another in three places— Paradise before the Fall; the Rocky Mountains before the wire fence; and the Declaration of Independence" (119). Perhaps Wister himself sensed the prejudiced cynicism of age settling upon him and secretly yearned for the egalitarianism that his patrician background denied him.

Certainly *Lin McLean* is full of much of this nostalgic sense of a better world passing, a lament for a freer, less restrictive society, framed symbolically as always for the Bible-reading Wister in terms of the Garden of Eden. The opening lines of the novel define its setting as "the old days, the happy days when Wyoming was a Territory with a future instead of a state with a past, and the unfenced cattle grazed upon her ranges in prosperous thousands" (1). We sometimes forget when reading Wister's early Western writing what he never lets us forget in the later work—that he himself was looking wistfully back over a decade or more from the perspective of the 1890s into the 1880s. By the time *The Virginian* was published, the gap between writer and subject would be a generation, and when Wister's last Western stories appeared in 1928 the perspective had stretched to nearly fifty years. Even the less perceptive characters in *Lin McLean* sense the best days of the West slipping from them. As Lin says to the narrator: "Some day we punchers will not be here. The living will be scattered, and the dead—well, they'll be all right. Have yu' studied the wire fence? It's spreading to catch us like nets do the salmon in the Columbia River. No more salmon, no more cow-punchers." "His words made me sad," the narrator says, "though I know that progress cannot spare land and water for such things" (174).

This sad sense of the transience of the West would not be as strong in *The Virginian,* but it would become the main motif of Wister's later stories. And if *Lin McLean* succeeds at all as an integrated novel rather than as a collection of interrelated short stories, it is perhaps because of its ability to project this very consciousness of mutability in man and in society. Certainly, Lin "grows up" in this book, passing from irresponsible youth to a mature acceptance of his role in a social world. Similarly, the West of his young manhood is passing, yielding to a structured, "civilized" society. Wister, with his Spencerian philosophy of progress, his rigid Philadelphia social codes, and his elitist intellectual and aesthetic standards, must in the final analysis stamp the change with approbation. But, as with the opening lines on "the old days, the happy days," he senses the loss, as does the reader. We wonder whether Lin's journey into adulthood, and into the arms of the wooden Jessamine, is a progress at all. Late in the novel, at the biscuit-shooter's grotesque funeral, the grown-up Lin views the wild, heedless cowboys with mature eyes and says to the governor, "It feels like I was looking at ten dozen Lin McLeans." We cannot help wondering if he secretly didn't like the old Lin better.

Chapter Five

The Virginian

A Tale of Sundry Adventures

Those who read *The Virginian* today may find themselves wondering what all the excitement was about. It has become such an aphorism that the novel was the prototype for the modern Western that we might expect to find all the stock features of the genre. Some are there: the strong, silent hero; the dude tenderfoot; the schoolmarm heroine; boisterous southwestern humor; the endless panorama of lonely, beautiful land and sky; the climactic shoot-out while the town holds its breath. But in terms of the major elements of novels—characterization, style, plot, narrative point of view, and projection of philosophy—*The Virginian* is sui generis.

In fact, it is hardly a novel at all. Wister himself said that a reader looking carefully could see the scissor marks of the author's cut-and-paste job.[1] He worked seven distinct and virtually unedited and intact short stories, all previously published, into *The Virginian,* and each of these is thematically complete. They have little in common but the western setting and the character of the Virginian. Understandably, Wister's prepublication subtitle for the novel was "A Tale of Sundry Adventures," for which he substituted "A Horseman of the Plains" for the first edition, doubtless already sensitive to charges that the book was episodic and fragmented. Actually, to call *The Virginian* a collection of adventures was also puffery. The novel has moments of high drama, but essentially it is a collection of vignettes, and a close look at the plot will demonstrate how unadventurous most of the book is.

All the novel is ostensibly told by an unnamed narrator, a young mannered easterner who visits Wyoming periodically in the 1880s, providing an intermittent account of the exotic life he finds there. Wister had already developed this narrative voice in sections of *Lin McLean* and a number of other stories, and this narrator was to become a major character in nearly all Wister's Western writing that followed *The Virginian*. Although he is not so important that the novel becomes, as the *Encyclopaedia Britannica* maintains, "a humorous account of the misadventures of an easterner in Wyoming,"[2] his character is crucial to the book's development, and misunderstandings of *The Virginian* frequently arise from regarding it as entirely the hero's book. The narrator is a rather precious tenderfoot at the story's beginning who is overwhelmed by the strangeness, beauty, wildness, and strength of western life, which, despite its roughness, he finds admirable. From the first page, he is impressed by a young cowboy, also dramatically nameless, called the Virginian, who becomes the narrator's guide figure, helping him to grow into western life and values. Under the Virginian's tutelage, or at least following his example, the narrator slowly loses his vulnerability and naivete, developing the rugged self-sufficiency and moral common sense of the cowboy. At this level, and it is an important one often neglected by critics, *The Virginian* is simply a *bildungsroman*.

At the opening of the novel, the visiting narrator finds himself dumped off his train in Medicine Bow for a visit to the Sunk Creek Ranch of Judge Henry, a venerable cattleman and figure of respect and authority in the Wyoming Territory of 1884. What the man is doing in this half-tamed wilderness, his antecedents, and his relation to Judge Henry are a bit vague, and this vagueness persists throughout the book. However, from his pontificating during lulls in the action, we soon realize that this narrator is an opinionated, self-styled aristocrat, a rigid upholder of high social and moral standards, and a man with a code of professionalism and a regard for quality of any kind bordering on mania. Still, since we know almost nothing of his background, it is tempting simply to read Wister himself into the character; many critics have done so, and a few have been so rash as to refer mistakenly to the unnamed figure as "Wister."[3]

On the first page, from his incoming train, the narrator sees the Virginian in a trackside corral, a man "with the undulations of a tiger, smooth and easy, as if his muscles flowed beneath his skin."[4] The glittering stranger ropes a pony no other cowboy could, and a passenger comments, "That man knows his business." The remark is critical to an understanding of the Virginian's virtue and to the narrator's eventual unbounded admiration for the man. As the hero will later explain, "Now back East you can be middling and get along. But if you go to try a thing in this Western country, you've got to do it *well*" (243).

The narrator discovers that this "slim young giant, more beautiful than pictures," is the man Judge Henry has sent to escort him to Sunk Creek Ranch, some 260 miles away. First the two spend the night in Medicine Bow, and we see several more exhibitions of the Virginian's worth: he uses craft to trick a sleazy drummer out of a bed for the night, sex-appeal and gentlemanly tact to seduce a pretty boardinghouse owner (Wister forebears recounting particulars, of course), skill to win money in a poker game, and a boisterous bonhomie to lead the town in Rabelaisian revelry which he instantly quiets with a wave of his hand, like Casey at the bat, when he finds it is disturbing a sick woman. The most famous scene in the book, and perhaps in all American literature, involves the card game and further demonstrates the man's understated but magnetic mastery of all he surveys. Casually called a son of a bitch by the slimy, eponymously named saddle bum Trampas,

the Virginian's pistol came out, and his hand lay on the table, holding it unaimed. And with a voice as gentle as ever, the voice that sounded almost like a caress, but drawling a very little more than usual, so that there was almost a space between each word, he issued his orders to the man Trampas:—

"When you call me that, *smile.*" And he looked at Trampas across the table.

Yes, the voice was gentle. But in my ears it seemed as if somewhere the bell of death was ringing. (23)

It is, but it will not toll for Trampas for another few hundred pages.

In the meantime, the Virginian takes the narrator to Sunk Creek, "swallowed in the vast solitude of Western scenery." The sweeping beauty and massive purity of the West are inspirational, and the narrator feels that "every breath that I breathed was pure as water and strong as wine," as Wister gives us the first of the novel's several extended appreciations of the land. At the ranch, the Virginian finds himself assigned to look after the helpless dude, and at first there is little communication between the two. The Virginian lapses into a gentlemanly silence that we will repeatedly find is his defense against distasteful situations. Eventually, though, the dude and the cowboy find a common ground for interest and discussion in the antics of a neurotic chicken named Em'ly; if this sounds a mite cutesy, it is.

Wister then skips ahead two years and returns his narrator to Wyoming on a second visit. Still a greenhorn, but a bit wiser in the ways of the West, he continues his account of the beauties of the landscape and the virtues of the Virginian. A new schoolmarm named Molly Wood has come to the area. She derives from old aristocratic New England stock that has fallen upon hard times, and the reader is never allowed to forget her breeding. Like the narrator, Molly has had a chance to be duly impressed by the Virginian before she even arrives. He gallantly rescued her from a flooded river and a drunken stage driver. When she tried to thank him, he pocketed her scented hand-kerchief as a remembrance and rode off without giving his name, leaving her heart aflutter. She has gotten a hold on herself, though, and is now resisting the blatant masculinity of her deliverer, feeling that her attraction to him is a challenge to her own substantial ego. The classic war between the sexes and Molly's inevitable capitulation becomes the main theme of the book, superseding both the education of the narrator and the heightening struggle between the hero and the forces of evil, represented by Trampas and his rustlers.

Near the end of this second visit, the Virginian again evidences the spontaneous, fun-loving side of the cowboy nature at a ranch party where he and Lin McLean, in a sort of bachelor protest against the domestic life that is claiming many of their friends, switch clothes on all the babies brought to the gathering, causing great confusion. Eventually, the Virginian confesses his guilt and is naturally forgiven, because "they could not resist the way in which he had looked round upon them."

The next episode takes place a year or so later in the late 1880s, when the narrator runs into the Virginian by accident in Omaha. The cowboy briefly left Judge Henry's employ the year before, feeling that his worth was unappreciated and being too much of a gentleman to sing his own praises. The Judge, realizing what a valuable man he has almost lost, has made the Virginian a temporary foreman chap-eroning the Sunk Creek ranch hands as they drive a herd east and then return by train. There are rumors of gold strikes along the re-turn route, and the Virginian is challenged with the prospect of his whole crew deserting to the mines. They are being tempted and goaded by Trampas, temporarily a Sunk Creek hand, in an effort to humiliate the Virginian. The cowboys grow restive under the hero's cool leadership, and it seems for a moment that his authority has been broken when Trampas tells a tall tale and the Virginian is caught believing it. Only hours later, however, the hero captivates not only Trampas and the rebellious cowhands but an entire trainload of stranded travelers with an absurd, inflated story about the profits to be made from "frog ranching" that outdoes Twain's "Jumping Frog" yarn. Trampas is scorned for his gullibility, and the consensus is that the Virginian is the champion of the tall tale as well as everything else. The penitent cowboys return to him like a flock of lost sheep to a kindly, competent shepherd.

For his work in delivering the crew, Judge Henry rewards the Virginian with a permanent foremanship. Trampas quits to take up a career rustling. In the meantime, in another amusing vignette occupying several chapters, the Virginian tricks a humorless visiting hellfire-and-damnation Presbyterian minister into abandoning his harangues to the ranch hands. The hero also pursues his suit of Molly Wood and launches himself on an ambitious course of self-education to make himself culturally and aesthetically worthy of her.

In the next episode, the narrator is absent, presumably back East pursuing his other life, but Wister allows him to narrate the whole thing omnisciently anyway. First comes a story that originally appeared as "Balaam and Pedro" in *Harper's* in 1894, the account of a trip through rough country by the Virginian and a brutal rancher named Balaam who takes out his bad temper on his horse, Pedro. The Virginian is disgusted by Balaam's cruelty, but he observes one aspect of the code of the West, which is that you don't tell another man how to handle his stock, until Balaam savagely gouges out one of Pedro's eyes, at which point the hero methodically beats Balaam until he is "a blurred, dingy, wet pulp" and then binds up his wounds.

The "Balaam and Pedro" chapter provides an interesting insight into Wister's rewriting and censoring process when he worked material into the final novel of *The Virginian*. When the story had originally appeared nearly a decade earlier, Wister had been graphically and gruesomely specific about the eye gouging. Roosevelt, who often praised Wister's writing, had objected to the unsavory details and begged Wister to delete them. At first Wister demurred, but by the time of publication he had come around. He dedicated the book to Roosevelt, inscribing it, "To Theodore Roosevelt: Some of these pages you have seen, some you have praised, one stands new-written because you blamed it." The moderating of Wister's early realistic impulses is characteristic of the writing of *The Virginian*, and Roosevelt's prudery undoubtedly had much to do with it. John Seelye goes so far as to maintain that Roosevelt was "the greatest influence shap-

ing Wister's West, responsible for the taming process by which his
realistic journal entries became romantic fiction."⁵ This is probably
an exaggeration—there were many forces moderating Wister's realism, not the least of which was doubtless his realization that the
courtship of the hero was aimed primarily at a feminine audience—
but the president's advice was obviously not without effect.

The Virginian and the chastised Balaam continue their journey,
but they become separated and the Virginian is attacked by Indians,
shot, and left for dead. Conveniently, he is discovered by Molly
Wood, out for an afternoon ride. Showing coolness, and courage,
Molly stays with him, determined to defend the fallen hero from further attack, and gets the now-delirious man to her cabin. To this
point Molly has resisted the Virginian's suit, although strongly attracted to him, because of his lack of family and formal education.
Nursing him through a long recovery, though, with the opportunity
to observe his grace under pressure, is too much for the schoolmarm.
Before the hero is back in the saddle, Molly has sent word to her
family in Bennington that she is engaged to a cowboy. They are, of
course, shocked, except for one crusty aunt who shares Molly's grit
and good sense.

The most dramatic, controversial, and best-written section of the
novel follows the Virginian's recovery. Horses and cattle are being
stolen throughout the territory, and as the Virginian tells Molly,
"Steps will have to be taken by somebody soon, I reckon." The narrator arrives a day early to meet the Virginian for a camping trip and
becomes an unwilling witness to those "steps." The Virginian is the
leader of a vigilante posse that has caught two of the rustlers and is
about to hang them. One of the rustlers turns out to be Steve, an old
friend of the Virginian. The narrator is disturbed, not only by his
friend's willingness to hang Steve, but also by his apparent coolness
in doing so. In the morning, the men are hanged, although the narrator does not watch. He and the Virginian ride away from the stand
of cottonwoods where the deed was done. As they travel, the Virginian slowly reveals the depth of his pain over what he had to do.

The succeeding chapter, "The Superstition Trail," is perhaps the
best in the novel. Upset over Steve's necessary execution, the Virginian and the narrator find themselves riding a lonely high-country trail
that seems haunted with reproach. The Virginian is racked with
guilt, although he maintains, "I would do it all over again." Some of
Wister's most effective descriptions of scenery make the rugged coun-

try seem preternaturally ominous. They have been riding for hours when they realize that somewhere on the trail ahead are two men whose very presence in so isolated a place is suspect. After a couple of days of spooky cat-and-mouse with the unseen men, they hear a shot and soon find the body of Shorty, a ne'er-do-well cowhand whom the Virginian had befriended but who had foolishly fallen under the baleful influence of Trampas. The villain has obviously been the other mysterious man ahead on the trail and has shot Shorty to escape on the pair's only horse. Trampas does get away, and the Virginian cannot legally prove that he is the fugitive rustler or murderer of Shorty, but it is obvious that the simmering bad blood between the hero and the villain must soon boil.

In the penultimate section of the novel, it does. The Virginian and Molly ride to "town" (the only actual town named in the novel is Medicine Bow, at the beginning) for their wedding. By ill luck they are passed on the road by Trampas, spoiling for a fight. Molly sees it coming and begs the Virginian to ignore Trampas or ride away. He agrees, but then finds that Trampas has been drinking and boasting in the bars, accusing the Virginian of cowardice. The hero's friends, Lin McLean and Scipio Le Moyne, offer to take care of the saddle tramp for him, but his code demands that he meet the challenge himself. First, though, he goes to his friend, the Bishop of Wyoming, for advice. As a Christian the Bishop must counsel him to resist the temptation because of his promise to give his life to Molly. The Virginian answers him: "Yes; I have given it to her. But my life's not the whole of me. I'd give her twice my life—fifty—a thousand of 'em. But I can't give her—her nor anybody in heaven or earth—I can't give my—my—we'll never get at it, seh! There's no good in words. Good by." The Bishop says, "God bless him" (285).

The word, of course, that the Virginian was looking for in trying to explain what is more important than life is "honor," and he could not love Molly half as much if he did not love it more. So, with the blessing of everyone except his intended, he walks out looking for Trampas, who sneaks up on him and fires first, but is blown away by the Virginian's return fire. When he tells Molly he has killed his enemy, she says "Thank God!" and throws herself into his arms.

The dramatic destruction of Trampas would seem sufficient climax to the novel, but Wister adds a singular epilogue describing the Virginian and Molly's wedding journey and the Virginian's later trip east and conquest of Molly's family. This schmaltz is aimed straight at

female readers, and it does much to compromise the effect of some of
the book's realism.

The Hero with Two Faces

It should be clear from even so brief a sketch of the novel that integrity of plot is not its strength. Three main subplots thread hesi-
tantly through the book, bumping each other casually in a sort of
fictional Brownian movement. We can easily make out two of these:
the courtship narrative and the heightening conflict between the Virginian and Trampas. Except for the final showdown chapter, when
Molly begs her lover not to fight, these stories are almost totally un-
connected. The novel flip-flops back and forth from violent confrontation to comic romance, and there are not even transitional passages
to connect the world of Trampas with the world of Molly.

The courtship narrative divides itself tidily into four sections, sym-
metrically spaced throughout the novel: the arrival of Molly and the
beginning of the battle of the sexes with the Virginian; the Virginian's deliberate "culturing" of himself to become worthy of her; the
climax of the romantic action in which the Virginian recuperates under Molly's care and they plight their troth; and the last chapter describing the pastoral bliss of the wedding journey.

The struggle between hero and villain is also symmetrical. Trampas comes into the novel unequivocally damned: "There was in his
countenance the same ugliness that his words conveyed." We are told
this during his first episode, the famous card game, in which the Virginian earns his undying hatred. His second appearance is on the
train back from Omaha, when he tries to incite the Virginian's men
to desert and is bested in the telling of tall tales. A third section of
the novel very much concerning Trampas, although he is physically
absent, traces the rise of the rustler problem—we have no doubts that
Trampas is the leader of the gang from which the luckless Steve is
caught and hanged, and we also know that he is the murderer of
Shorty on the Superstition Trail. His final appearance is as the antag-
onist and eventual corpse in his showdown with the Virginian, the
only point in the book in which Molly's plot and Trampas's do not
go their separate ways.

There is a third type of "action," which might be called "sketches
of the Virginian." Much of the novel is really just a collection of
anecdotes about the Virginian in particular and life in the West in

general, interwoven with Wister's commentary on the significance of that character and life. In these sketches the hero appears in many guises: the masculine, spontaneous Virginian rollicking like a puppy in the streets of Medicine Bow; the whimsical, crackerbarrel philosopher Virginian commenting on the psychology of the hen Em'ly; the Peck's Bad Boy Virginian swapping babies at a ranch social; the crafty but sensible Virginian tricking the hellfire minister who tries to cow him with righteousness; the humane and righteous Virginian beating the bestial Balaam for blinding a horse; the authoritarian moralist Virginian upholding law and order as the leader of a lynch mob; and so on, through a hundred or more vignettes, some extended enough to claim status as full stories, others no more than a paragraph, but each illuminating the multifaceted character of this cowboy hero.

Perhaps the novel's greatest strength lies here. Incident by incident, Wister illuminates the various aspects of his hero until the final figure is more fully developed than any other in early Western fiction. Although he is a "character" in the Local Color tradition, he is less eccentric than most, except in his virtue, and far more substantial. Part of the stock-in-trade of Bret Harte, G. W. Cable, Joel Chandler Harris, Ambrose Bierce, and even Mark Twain in his weaker moments was the odd figure whose idiosyncrasies were often an exaggerated shorthand for the traits of the fictional region. Often, like some of Dickens's weaker caricatures, they were one-trick eccentrics—purely vicious like Simon Legree, insouciant like Harte's gambler Oakwood, rascally like Twain's duke and king. The Virginian's name, however, is Legion.

Preeminently, the Virginian is a substantial physical presence. This prototype for Gary Cooper and John Wayne literally stands tall, six-two. Much of his habitual understatement in speech is made possible by the effective overstatement of his physical appearance. Stature radiates from him, and the impact of his presence is attested to by every perceptive character in the novel. Men sense that he is not a man to be messed with. Women, like the boardinghouse keeper in Medicine Bow, breathe heavily and yield discreetly. The virginal Molly, before their marriage, stands trembling before his very picture. He is the epitome of that red-blooded health both Wister and Roosevelt found on fleeing the anemic East.

His substantiality in the present is accentuated by his lack of a past. From his beguiling namelessness to his lack of biography, he is the western "new man," asking to be taken for what he is and what he appears to be. He's not even really a Virginian, as Wister was well aware, for he wrote to his friend, the journalist Richard Harding Davis, "There's nothing typically Virginian about him, save some accent, some bad grammar, and some apparent laziness; and he was meant by me to be just my whole American creed in flesh and blood. . . . It was by design he continued nameless because I desired to draw a sort of heroic circle about him, almost a legendary circle and thus if possible create an illusion of remoteness."[6]

This very lack of roots detaches him from the corruption of the East and endows him with a mythic purity that might be less believable if the reader knew more of his past. His lover Molly, for all her virtue, shares some of the snobbish prejudices of her blue-blooded New England and must purge herself of them to form a more perfect union. He, though, is entirely a westerner because he is emphatically not anything else. Of his past, the narrator tells us only that he came from a big family, left home young, and has spent the intervening years wandering to and fro in the earth and up and down in it.

The correlative of the Virginian's overt physicality, his beauty, strength, and athletic grace, is the man's fundamental reserve. His obvious strength of body and character saves him from diffidence, but Wister repeatedly paints him as having an aristocratic introspection that sets him above the common run of cowboys. The hallmark of this reserve is his silence. He is not afraid of words, but he uses them deliberately and despises glibness. Several times Wister stresses his habit of falling into an almost morose silence after talk, as when he has bested Trampas with the tall tale of "frog ranching," and then, "the talking part of him deeply and unbrokenly slept." For him, both boasting and pleading betray weakness bordering on sin. He criticizes Browning's "Incident in the French Camp" because a brave and dying soldier says he's been killed, of which the Virginian comments, "Now a man who was man enough to act like he did, yu' see, would fall dead without mentioning it." Similarly, "he detested words of direct praise."

His silence and his modesty derive from a well of monumental self-confidence and self-respect. He always senses his worth and "felt himself to be a giant whom life had made 'broad gauge,' and denied opportunity." The novel is actually in large part about opportunity knocking in the form of Molly and the foremanship of Judge Henry's ranch, but even when he is a common cowpoke at the beginning, the Virginian knows that "the creature we call a *gentleman* lies deep in the hearts of thousands that are born without chance to master the outward graces of the type." The term *gentleman* subsumes for both the Virginian and his creator a panoply of virtues of which etiquette is the least important.

The most important is professionalism, the key to the character of the gentleman. In the case of the Virginian, it manifests itself in simple ability to outperform other men in virtually every phase of human activity. And not only is the man better than other men, but he knows it. Further, he makes that awareness a cardinal element in his moral code. Unlike some of Hemingway's more inarticulate heroes— the bullfighters, Ole Andreson, Harry Morgan—the Virginian does not exist simply in a world of pure sensory flow, behaving correctly by instinct but largely oblivious to the ethos of his behavior. He is, as critic John Williams points out, both the Emersonian Natural Man who functions by instinct, and one of the Calvinistic Elect of God who function by reason and are well aware of their moral status vis-à-vis their fellowmen.[7]

Casual readers of *The Virginian* may not notice how little of his superiority actually consists of mastery of the objective physical skills of the range—riding, roping, shooting—the skills of survival, both in terms of nature and of outlaws and Indians. No question, the Virginian is competent in these matters; from the opening scene taming the difficult horse to the final mano-à-mano defeat of Trampas, he bears out the book's opening comment on him—"That man knows his business." Still, the Virginian is a far cry from the simple men of James Fenimore Cooper's forest, or Vardis Fisher's mountain men. Natty Bumppo may be, to reverse Lowell's epithet, just an Indian daubed over with white, but the Virginian's skills far transcend primitive reflex. His real abilities, actually, are social. He is a master poker player, tall tale teller, bunkhouse lawyer. He can be the life of the party when he wants. He can outcon con men and outthink ministers in a religious talk. He has a flair for the dramatic, vanishing after rescuing Molly from the stage or ominously laying his pistol before him and commanding Trampas to "Smile!" He is an effective, but not ruthless, lover, knowing that the boardinghouse keeper can be won by a tip of the hat, but that for Molly he must learn Shakespeare. Naturally, he evidences the mind of a scholar and the memory of an actor when the occasion calls for it: at one point he recites from memory seven lines on *bees* from *Henry V,* when most people couldn't remember seven lines on kings.

The key to the Virginian's mastery of the puzzling manners and

mores of western society is superior perception, an ability to see
through appearances to the real meaning of things. Whether through
moral, gentlemanly instincts, or through an almost animal cunning,
Wister's westerner is able to penetrate to the truth underlying the
apparent chaos of western life and to manipulate that life effectively
by acting on his perception. The Virginian is not to be fooled or mis-
led, for "the sons of the sage-brush . . . live nearer nature, and they
know better." He does not scorn rational reason and, in its down-to-
earth form, common sense, but rather welcomes it, although instinctive insight is more important. James K. Folsom sees this insight as
the most important quality the Virginian shares with (or passed on
to) other western heroes: "That insight into the world which Wister
sees as the most significant quality possessed by the Western hero is
basic to the character of most other fictional Westerners, who are
conceived ultimately as men of insight, and whose success depends
upon their ability to see more deeply into the meaning of circumstances than their opponents."[8]

It is this superiority of insight that makes the Virginian not so
much *of* his society as superior to it and which lends to the novel
much of the mythic and epic quality that has fixed it in the American
imagination. It has also made the book controversial, for Wister is
saying that in the new world of the West the superior man must not
only be better than others, he must act on that superiority. It is not
so much that he is above the law as that he realizes that often there
is no law for him to be above, and he must make his own. The lynching of Steve and the killing of Trampas have been repeatedly attacked
by Wister's critics, who insist upon generalizing Wister's observa-
tions concerning justice and anarchy in a particular situation—one
that Wister himself insistently points out is unique. Leslie Fiedler's
diatribe in *The Return of the Vanishing American* is typical: "But behind
the talk of honesty and chivalry, it is personal violence, taking the
law into one's own hands, for which *The Virginian*—along with all of
its recastings and imitations right down to *High Noon*—apologizes.
The duel and the lynching represent its notions of honor and glory;
and the images of these have occupied the center of the genteel or
kitsch Western ever since, in pulp magazines, in hardcover or paper-
back books, on radio, TV, or in the movies."[9]

Fiedler, for all his brilliance as a psychological critic, shows his
limitations as a social one, because he fails to take circumstances into
account—the circumstances that Wister insists, and demonstrates

through his painstaking delineation of subject, are at the very heart of his art. John K. Milton, a pedestrian writer, is closer to the mark when he points out that "when the Virginian changes from a soft-talking, gentle man into a brutal avenger, it is only because justice demands it."[10] The Virginian is what he is—a killer—because of the world in which he lives, not in spite of it. His moral imperatives, borrowed by Wister from the prelegalistic medieval world, derive from an Augustinian conception of transcendent (or divine) law made manifest to a moral elect and through them imposed upon a society that has not yet generated law. The Virginian does not overthrow law and order; he creates it in a primitive form.

The obvious flaw in this interpretation of Wister's moral vision is that Trampas might just as well have won the famous gunfight. In fact, he had a better chance, since he shot first—once again incompetence is equated with immorality. It is exactly this point that moves the novel from the realm of realistic art to that of romantic wish fulfillment. Had the Virginian lost the shoot-out, or had Molly rejected him for fighting as she promised, or had he degenerated morally in a psychologically realistic fashion à la Hawthorne after killing a man, the novel might have gained enormously as a serious moral statement. But it would have never been one of the best-selling American novels of all time, reworked again and again to lead the reader to the same, masturbatory self-satisfying climax.

The ending of *The Virginian* was resolved to satisfy the reader and the author. Wister leads us with considerable skill to believe in a thoroughly established character and in the morally ambivalent and threatening world in which he lives. He convinces us that that world, the frontier West, is a different world with new rules and demanding a new kind of hero, equipped with special skills of reflex, insight, and survival. He places that hero at a moment of potentially tragic decision. The Virginian must opt for love, order and civilization, sacrificing honor and self-respect, or he must commit himself to either death or the loneliness of heroism. Wister gives him the best of both decisions, adding a "happily ever after" epilogue that explains that the Virginian becomes rich, founds a dynasty, and lives a long life.

Why did Wister, a serious artist and a conscientious craftsman, do this? Why did he bring his novel to a point at which, like Conrad, he could have delineated the genuine implications of moral decision, and then let his hero off the hook, telling the reader that morality has no painful price? The answer is the reason *The Virginian* sold and sold and sold: it was what the casual reader wanted to read. More important, it was what Wister wanted to write.

Even an armchair psychologist can see in the Virginian a synthesis of virtues that Wister found so disturbingly irreconcilable in his own life. Conscious from childhood of a lack of spontaneity in himself, resenting overrefinement yet yielding to it, Wister was a Philadelphia hothouse flower powerfully drawn to the natural, primitive life of Wyoming. There man was a more atavistic and instinctive animal than he could ever be on the Main Line. When it came to creating a hero, Wister wanted one with an animality of an almost naturalistic nature. This is one pole of the Virginian's nature—physical prowess, elemental personal magnetism, primal instincts, all producing not only survival but dominance in the jungle of the American frontier. The Virginian is an instinctive beast at home in his primitive environment.

His other face, though, is that of the Philadelphia society that Wister had fled—reserved, courtly, controlled, and most of all, discriminatory. The Virginian, like his creator, is compelled to weigh the moral consequences of every decision. Thus, the agony of choosing between Molly's love and honor. It was an agony that Wister was quite willing and able to work up. What he could not face was subjecting his beloved hero to the painful consequences of that decision, one way or the other. John G. Cawelti in his study of popular fiction *Adventure, Mystery, and Romance* acknowledges the compromise that lessened *The Virginian* as art, but made it eminently successful: "*The Virginian* brings together in harmony a number of conflicting forces or principles in American life and this synthesis and resolution of conflicting values is a literary exemplification of the principle of having your cake and eating it too. Wister's characters, actions, and setting have a surface verisimilitude, but it is a moral fantasy that shapes character and action. Thus a reader can enjoy a world in which things work out just as he wishes them to without any sense that this world is overly artificial or contrived."[11] As H. L. Mencken noted, nobody ever lost money underestimating the taste of the American people. Ironically, this rule-of-thumb applies particularly aptly to the most significant novel by a man who surely never overestimated it.

Chapter Six

Later Western Fiction

Members of the Family: The Land of Lost Content

The 1911 publication of *Members of the Family* did not mark absolutely the end of Wister's career as a writer of fiction, for seventeen years later he would pull together one more volume of stories. But with that exception his waning energies in the last quarter-century of his life would be directed elsewhere. Wister was just short of fifty when he completed the last story for *Members of the Family,* and more major fiction might have been expected of him. But an increasing interest in politics and civic affairs, the death of his wife, and a deepening concern with World War I and international problems distracted him through his fifties.

Even *Members of the Family* really stood not so much at the end of Wister's Western fiction as beyond it. The groundwork for several of these stories had been laid before *The Virginian's* success was truly established. Wister wrote "In the Back" in the early summer of 1902 when *The Virginian* was starting to climb the best-seller lists,[1] and the key episode in "Timberline" was drawn almost intact from an essay Wister had written in 1899.[2] Many of the characters—Scipio Le Moyne, Specimen Jones, Uncle Pasco, and other "members of the family"— are drawn from earlier writing. Significantly, until his 1910 trip, Wister had not actually been West since his honeymoon in 1898, and therefore the material for the later stories was largely drawn from notebook entries that grew more dated with each passing year. With the lengthening distance between author and subject, a new tone comes to dominate the writing. From the first, Wister was concerned with capturing a vanishing frontier in fiction, and so a wistful quality characterizes even his earliest stories. With *Members of the Family* the air of nostalgia becomes pervasive. In case we miss it in the stories themselves, Wister opens the collection with a long, bittersweet preface lamenting the lost past: "Time steps in between the now that is and the then that was with a vengeance; it blocks the way for us all; we cannot go back."³ In the manner of all romantic writers, however, who tell us that we can't return, Wister bears us back ceaselessly into the past.

What Wister sees destroying the old West and supplanting it is civilization of a sort. It comes in a variety of forms: the Indian reservation, the cavalry post, a country store, a schoolmarm, a nagging wife. All have appeared before in Wister's stories, but in *Members of the Family* they set the tone. The freedom, the spontaneity, the wildness are giving way at every turn. Wister's omnipresent narrator never lets us forget what's being lost, and the sense of poignancy so thickens in spots that it threatens to overwhelm the narrative: "I loved that country," says the narrator in "The Gift Horse," "and sometimes it seems as if I must go there and smell the sage-brush again—or die."⁴ The setting of *Members of the Family* is the land of Wister's lost content—"the happy highways where I went and cannot come again."

This tone of regret is all the more remarkable because, of the eight stories in the collection, six are straightforward comedy without even the dark overtones of Twain or Bierce. The central character in all but one of these, "In the Back," is Scipio Le Moyne, who readers of *The Virginian* will remember as the bluffest of the Sunk Creek cowboys and the hero's closest friend. By turns garrulous and taciturn, outrageous or stoically understated, Scipio combines the bluster of the *miles gloriosus* with the cool professionalism and fundamental decency that Wister outlined as Saxon traits in "The Evolution of the Cowboy." If less commanding than the Virginian, Scipio is also less wooden, a more human representative of the cowboy than his knightly friend.

In the opening story, "Happy-Teeth," Scipio gets the best of a venal, scheming Indian agent. The story is vintage Wister. Nearly killed breaking a wild horse, Scipio finds himself confined to a hospital on an Indian reservation. He is displeased to learn the assistant clerk at the agency store is a slimy character, Horace Pericles Byram, called "Horacles," whose uncle is a U.S. senator, corrupt to the core like all Wister politicians. Placed in charge of the company store while recuperating, the reliable Scipio suspects Horacles of scheming to defraud the Indians. A bit of chicanery and his uncle's influence make it possible for Horacles to set up a rival store and undercut the agency by selling cheap goods illegally procured. Scipio is fit to bust, for his sense of responsibility makes him feel responsible for the agency store, and his pride is outraged by the thought that the venal Horacles has outfoxed him. On the day Horacles is to open his rival store, Scipio convinces him that the event will be enlivened if he performs some magic tricks for the Indians. Horacles does and concludes his act by belching fire and producing his false teeth on the end of his tongue. The horrified Indians bolt in panic and never return, afraid of the white man's magic.

Wister has worked the material of "Happy-Teeth" before, of course; the white man's cleverness overcoming the Indians' superstition, the venal manipulator outwitted by a cowboy's skill, the roaring antics of southwestern humor, and the hero's deep concern for professionalism and responsibility. There are three major characters from the Wister repertory company, too: Le Moyne, the Virginian, and the narrator. The Virginian is as always grave, laconic, solicitous of his injured friend, full of humble wisdom about the evil of politicians, and scornful of "immodest men" (Horacles). The narrator of "Happy-Teeth" is less in evidence, and he assumes more importance in later stories in the collection. But he too is as he has always been—scholarly, itinerant, a bit formal, and always an outsider. He is less of a greenhorn than we saw him in *The Virginian* and some of the earlier stories, notably "A Pilgrim on the Gila," but he is still distinctly not a native westerner. Le Moyne calls him "Professor" as he did in *The Virginian,* and the cowboys, except the trashy ones who scorn him, still treat him with a bemused politeness. They all welcome him as a friend, occasionally seek his knowledge of the abstruse, but always make him aware that it is *their* West, and he is a visitor.

"Spit-Cat Creek," the second story, is an obvious companion to "Happy-Teeth," but its analogue is "The Jimmyjohn Boss," that story of Dean Drake's youthful trial by fire taming an anarchic trail camp through courage and wit. Scipio Le Moyne is the neophyte this time, trusted by the Virginian to deliver the payroll to cowboys on a line crew. Overwhelmed by his responsibility, he vows not only to deliver the money, but to keep anyone from knowing he has it. However, the slimy Uncle Pasco, the peddler, trader, and roving bunko artist of "The Jimmyjohn Boss," guesses from Scipio's uncommon sobriety that he has the money. Uncle Pasco gets the drop on him and steals it, but Scipio tricks him into fleeing by a trail that doubles back on itself, and he recovers the payroll. Between loss and recovery, Scipio goes through appropriate fulminations of self-recrimination for allowing Uncle Pasco to outwit him, and we see again the conscious-stricken burden of responsibility that hangs heavy on all Wister heroes. "Spit-Cat Creek" is a bit more ambitiously structured than the average Wister story, for imbedded in it is a long letter from Scipio to the Virginian that dovetails neatly into the plot and allows Wister to produce a little gem of cowboy rhetoric. The letter opens, "Dear friend: I got no dictionery but if any of my spelling raises your suspicions you can borrow a dictionery at your end and theirby correct my statements which are otherwise garranteed to be strictly accurite." Uncle Pasco is of the humorous-garrulous-slimy-villain variety rather than the nonhumorous-laconic type like Trampas, and there is a good bit of bantering between him and Scipio, leaving the tone of the story comic throughout.

If the tone of "Spit-Cat Creek" is comic, that of "In the Back" is farcical. Wister acknowledged drawing heavily on Kipling for his military stories,[5] and none shows that influence more directly than this, which in plot and tone could have come right out of *Plain Tales from the Hills*. "In the Back" opens with an acidic portrait of a politically minded and thoroughly hypocritical secretary of war who tries to curry favor with a bunch of redneck army recruits by picturing himself as the defender of their rights and assuring them that they are as good as their officers, if not better. Despite "sensible" counseling by our old friend Sergeant Specimen Jones, the recruits believe the secretary's promise to "stand behind them." Furthermore, the man's rabble-rousing foments discontent among the troops, who would otherwise have known their place and been perfectly happy with their Spartan lives. One recruit, a naive boy named Leonidas Bateau, becomes overly familiar with the wife of the fort's commandant, Captain Stone. She is nineteen, and her forty-five-year-old husband is hypersensitive to the age difference. As the narrator says, "When you see a wife of nineteen playing the organ for a trooper of twenty-two and a husband of forty-five constantly remarking that a man is always as young as he feels, why, then you are at no great distance from comedy, and the joke draws nearer when the wife is anxious that the trooper should not feel the want of his mother, and the trooper retains the limpid innocence of the watermelon."[6] Leonidas calls for the captain's wife one day, casually inquiring for "Sister Stone." The commandant explodes, literally kicking the young man out. Feeling hard used, Leonidas makes a fool of himself petitioning the secretary of war for justice. When none comes, he quits the army in disgust. Some time later the secretary visits the territory. At a whistle stop, Leonidas, now a cowboy, kicks him in the butt and escapes on horseback. Overall, this is the weakest story in *Members of the Family,* a slightly developed social sketch which Wister uses as a vehicle for a lesson on the evils of egalitarianism.

"Extra Dry" is another story of Scipio Le Moyne, this time fallen on hard times and referred to as "Bellyful"—not until the end of the story do we find out that the hard-luck hobo of Scipio's story is himself a few years earlier and much less prosperous. Chicanery and one-upmanship again spin the plot. Unable to find work, Scipio is literally starving in a cowtown whose citizens are being victimized by a traveling shell-game huckster. Watching the man's sleight of hand carefully, Scipio satisfies himself that the con artist is cheating. Once he is sure he's dealing with a crook, Scipio feels licensed to fight fire with fire, in this case to steal from a thief. He ambushes the shell-game man and relieves him of his ill-gotten gains, which serve Scipio as a grubstake for a fresh start in life. The narrator, when Scipio finishes the story, is horrified. He is a writer and wants to write the story, but change the closing theft. Scipio sticks to his guns: if the narrator writes the story, he demands, he must tell it as it was without sugarcoating it. Wister concludes "Extra Dry" with this passage, which tells us a good deal about his attitudes toward art, philosophy, and life. The narrator speaks:

"Well—I don't like the way Bellyful just went off and prospered and—"
"But he did."
"And never felt sorry or—"
"But he didn't."
"Well—"
"D'you claim he'd oughtn't? Think of him! Will y'u please to think of him after that shell game? Begging honest work and denied all over, everywhere, till his hat and his clothes and his boots were in holes, and his body was pretty near in holes—think of him, just a kind of hollo' vessel of hunger lying in that stable while the shell-game cheat goes off with his pockets full of gold." Scipio spoke with heat.
"Yes, I know. But, if Bellyful afterward could only feel sorry and try—"
"Are you figuring to fix that up?"—he was still hotter—"because I forbid you to monkey with the truth. Because I *never* was sorry."
"What?"
"I was Bellyful," said Scipio, becoming quiet. "Yes, that was eight years ago." He mused still more, his eyes grew wistful. "I was nineteen then. God, what good times I have had!"[7]

Scipio's next story, "Where it Was," lacks the serious overtones of "Extra Dry." This is Scipio's bucolic reminisence about the Edenic way it was in Washington's Thowmet Valley (Wister honeymooned in the actual Methow Valley), when fine folks loved each other and lived in harmony. The main "characters" are Frisco Baldy and Kultus Jake, a pair of much-traveled, grizzled but affable reprobates—gruff, time-worn soldiers of fortune from the early days of western adventuring. The two are rough and cantankerous, but secretly devoted to each other. They are also miserly and unfortunately own the only patch of land in town suitable for building a schoolhouse for the use of another incarnation of Molly Wood, Miss Carey. A subplot develops her rocky romance with the flinty young owner of the town's only store. Jake and Baldy make a last feeble effort to go hunting, fall to fighting with each other, return to town, acknowledge their mutual affection, and shortly die, leaving the land to the town. Miss Carey and Mr. Edmund marry after a sentimental funeral for the two old cusses who are planted under a common board, reading "Their heart was free from malice, and all their anger was excess of love." The treacle is utterly without Blakean subtlety, though, and this is one of Wister's weaker stories. Scipio, who tells the story to the narrator, can't stand too much gushing: "Oh, yes, their happiness filled that store, filled the whole cabin, crowded it. Maybe that's why I left the valley." Perhaps, like his creator, he was becoming increasingly lugubrious and was moving on to sadder stories.

The last story of *Members of the Family,* however, is pure fluff and not very good fluff, either. "The Drake Who Had Means of His Own" is a drawing-room comedy and closet drama set in a Wyoming cabin around 1910. The narrator, again indistinguishable from the author, is "duding" on a small ranch of a young former cowboy, Jimmy Culloden, newly married. Jimmy is a good-hearted, ex-hell-raiser of the Lin McLean variety, but now a "stable citizen, an anchored man, county commissioner, selling vegetables, alfalfa and taking in paying boarders."[8] He is also henpecked, and the narrator, sympathizing with his plight, calls his attention to the ranch pond where a drake "disciplines" his two female ducks by constantly keeping them guessing as to where he will go—into the pond, back to the barn, ad infinitum. Jimmy gets the message, lets his nagging wife worry about his whereabouts for a time, and the woman is cured. Jimmy and the narrator exchange winks. The story has all the coyness of the "Em'ly" story in *The Virginian*—lots of cuteness about bird behavior, but there are serious overtones of regret for the lost wildness of the frontier. It was a regret that was to become far more bitter in Wister's last book of fiction, *When West Was West.*

When West Was West: Drear Dead Days

Thirteen declining years of Wister's old age passed between the writing of the last story of *Members of the Family* in 1911 and work on the first of *When West Was West* in 1924.[9] In contrast to the long, intensely personal preface to the earlier book, Wister wrote none for the second, published in 1928; perhaps by that time, confrontation with the subject of the West outside fiction was too painful. If the stories of the previous book pointed the way to western decline, the stories of the later one look back upon it. This last view at the territory is actually looking at the West long after it "was West," a generation or more after the closing of the frontier. The streams are fished out, the elk and the antelope gone, and the Indians have been reduced to picture-postcard parodies of their former nobility. Whores, pimps, charletons, con men, hypocrites teem in the seedy, ugly towns. A few pathetic relics of the early cowboy days live out their lives, raging against the new rotten world or resigned to it. A decrepit "civilization" has superseded the fresh anarchy of the past in a variety of forms: Victorian prudery and hypocrisy, quack medicine, pseudoscience, corrupt politics, and the infirmities of pointless old age. Systematically Wister takes the character types of his early stories and etches their sad transformation into the "new" West. The Indian, the cowboy, the doctor, the soldier, the hunter, the rancher, the preacher, and even the dude—all reappear in diminished and cheapened forms in these sad stories.

The Indian suffers the worst. Wister came West in 1885 too late to see the Indian in anything like his primal splendor, but the red men in his early stories have a considerable nobility. The Indian of the decade between 1910 and 1920, however, was all but plowed under, a vestigial reminder of what he had been before his last pathetic battles of a generation earlier. Wister sketches his plight in two of these stories. "Bad Medicine" is about a dispossessed Shoshone prince, Sun Road, a grandson of the last Shoshone chief, who "had no inheritance to leave his descendants, except the inevitable extinction of his whole race." Proud and superstitious, Sun Road stays aloof from the white man, still dressing in his feathery finery and playing beautifully on his Indian pipe, by which Wister, the old music major, indicates the Indian's sensitivity and primitive superiority. The narrator, now a prosperous easterner looking for a guide in the Yellowstone country, persuades Sun Road to take him there and softens the Indian's hauteur by befriending his young son. Slowly, Sun Road overcomes his fear of the "white man's magic" and allows himself to be photographed. His vanity gets the best of him, and soon he is cravenly posing for tourists in Yellowstone Park, the forerunner of the Hollywood Indian. His debasement is short-lived, though, for he agrees to pose for flash pictures before the crater of Old Faithful. The geyser erupts, the flash goes off, Sun Road panics, rushes madly onto dangerous ground, and vanishes into the sulphurous earth. The abrupt death is disconcerting because the tone of the story has been one of bemusement, but the tragedy is real. The Indian, first dispossessed by the white man, is debased by a tinsel culture's appeal to the Indian's pride, and then destroyed when superstition reasserts itself in the face of white technology and knowledge of nature.

Another Indian story, "Absalom and Moulting Pelican," finds the red man in a state of total decrepitude and does a thorough job on the image of the frontier preacher as well. Although the story is straight southwestern humor, its world is as bleak as any Wister ever painted. The setting is a blistering desert cavalry post in Arizona where heat and boredom are enough to warp the mind. As one character says: "In this glorious territory, Mother Nature is a freak. . . . Beneath her influence I have become a freak with all the rest of the population." The freakiest are a couple of local color characters, the Reverend Xanthus Merrifew ("Absalom") and his protégé Moulting Pelican, a lonely, deranged, threadbare old Apache who follows Absalom around like a dog. The preacher dresses like a hippie and incessantly inflicts upon the captive audience of the post his theory that the Indians are one of the lost tribes of Israel. He coaches Moulting Pelican to speak before the visiting secretary of war (whom we've met before), declaring his Hebraic ancestry, but the narrator, Doc Leonard, and a frontier Brom Bones named Hugh Lloyd boobytrap the speech, so the poor Indian accidentally snatches off Absalom's flowing wig. Moulting Pelican flees in terror, thinking he has somehow scalped the parson, who is himself guffawed out of town.

Wister is not content with just the cream of the jest, and he has the terrified Indian return to his white protectors, upon whom he is totally dependent. Soon thereafter the cavalry and Doc Leonard leave the benighted base in torpor. A fascinating footnote to "Absalom and Moulting Pelican" is that it contains one of American literature's earliest treatments of hashish, a three-page description of its use by Doc Leonard and Hugh Lloyd to ward off boredom. The account is so ably accurate that we suspect that Wister tried the drug himself or consulted someone with firsthand knowledge of it.

A less successful portrait of post life, perhaps because it is a less dismal one, is "Captain Quid," an overly long story of a cavalry officer married to a stong-minded woman determined to break him of smoking. To avoid detection, Captain Monk takes to chewing rather than puffing, a habit he hides from his wife who smugly believes she knows everything about him. He saves his life one day by spitting tobacco juice in the eye of a rattlesnake, after which he proudly lights up in public. As with "In the Back" and "Napoleon Shave-Tail," Wister devotes much space to establishing the reader's feel for the petty gossip of an army base, and although his dialogue among the base women is not without humor, the thin plot doesn't justify the story's length. The overall picture, though, fits that of the rest of *When West Was West,* for the army that we find here is the thoroughly domesticated one of the last days of the frontier. Interestingly, "Captain Quid" contains one of Wister's few historical inaccuracies. [10]

One of Wister's most peculiar stories is "Lone Fountain." The protagonist is a prematurely aged trapper, Kenneth Scott, an archetypal "natural man" in the Rousseauistic sense. Illegitimate son of a wandering gentleman, superb natural athlete, skilled hunter and trapper with the instincts of an Indian or a wild beast, he is one of several characters Wister drew who approaches the Jack London model of man as a successful animal. Although a sensitive and intelligent man, a reader of poetry and Shakespeare, Scott claims to be a complete rationalist with neither understanding nor sympathy for love, religion, mystery, or romance. Wister the romantic writer deals him a comeuppance, of course. Scott hires on as guide to a German geologist whose passionate Greek wife still worships nature gods. Scott falls in love, still scoffing at her gods, until one night when the two are about to consummate their love: a geyser erupts (the "lone fountain") and, to Scott's horror, the god Apollo appears in the steam and carries the woman away. The story is one of the most complex Wister ever attempted. The conflict between rationality and mysticism and the exploration of the meaning of love and eroticism are seriously undertaken, and it is one of the few Wister stories without a trace of humor. Unfortunately, Scott is more an exotic caricature than a character, and the fantastic ending is too abrupt an injection of the supernatural to be convincing. The final image of the mountain man ten years after the apparition is effective, though—gray and broken, a shell of the glorious child of nature he had been, serving as a slightly "touched" guide for tourists. Whether the story works on a philosophical level, it is a convincing picture of another western type in decline. It is perhaps not stretching it to see "the god Apollo" as something akin to Algernon Blackwood's Wendigo, the spirit of the wilderness that destroys its worshipers.

"Once Round the Clock" is the first of three stories in *When West Was West* about the degeneracy of Texas and Texans. The protagonist is young Doc Leonard, an idealistic Bostonian who falls among thieves on the Staked Plains. He has hung out his shingle in a county tyrannized by a sinister female root doctor who keeps the locals in thrall through a combination of occult hocus-pocus and an alliance with the local criminal element. One of Wister's most fascinating characters, Dr. Salamanca is a frontier Morgan Le Fay who in true lamia tradition lures handsome young "assistants" into her bower of bliss, seduces them and saps their moral strength, and then casts them off and has them killed when she tires of them. She practices "medicine" from a consulting room that features a stuffed crocodile, and most of her cures involve spells. Doc Leonard offers a less exotic but more effective healing, but he is no match for his rival, who vows to kill him. She arranges a blasting "accident" that would have worked if not for the timely intervention of Leonard's friend and adviser, Colonel Steptoe McDee, who advises his protégé to get out of town while he can. The story closes with Doc Leonard packing his bags.

Colonel Steptoe is the last of Wister's fully developed western characters, the successor to Lin McLean, the Virginian, and Scipio Le Moyne. Unlike them, he is no longer young and vigorous. A southern aristocrat and Confederate officer, he lost everything in the Civil War and went west to start over. *When West Was West* picks him up after the turn of the century, his health decaying, his old cowboy friends dead or gone, bitterly watching the once-free open range fill up with trashy people with trashy morals. McDee is blustery and bombastic, but brave and cunning, and possessed of a ramrod morality and a will of iron. Fierce and feisty in his decline, he is the apotheosis of those dispossessed rebels Wister created more than a third of a century earlier in "The Second Missouri Compromise."

McDee's long resistance to Dr. Salamanca's corruption of Texas is resolved in "Little Old Scaffold," a story set some time after Doc Leonard's departure. By this time, Salamanca has had several of her critics killed from ambush, and nearly all McDee's supporters have followed Doc Leonard's example and left the county. Salamanca is preparing to seize political control with the corrupt politician Jinks Flemming as her stalking-horse. Flemming is the epitome of the Wister villain—slick, cheap, hail-fellow-well-met, a salesman, and a manipulator. In the last showdown of Wister's fiction, McDee calls home the little band of brothers who still back him. Publicly debunking Flemming's claim to Civil War heroism, McDee exposes the man just before the election. McDee is shot by an unseen assassin, Flemming flees in disgrace, and Dr. Salamanca is killed by her frustrated followers. McDee dies happy, knowing that he has, at least temporarily, returned decency to Texas.

There is little decency of any kind in the third Texas story, "Skip to My Lou," one of Wister's best and bitterest tales. It examines with candor the seamy life of postfrontier society, exposing Victorian small-town hypocrisy on a level that might have made Sinclair Lewis blush. The setting is the general West Texas locale of "Once Round the Clock" and "Little Old Scaffold" before the action of those two stories, and Doc Leonard and Colonel Steptoe McDee are only observers of the narrative. The wide-open, free cowtowns have given way to provincialism under the thumb of Mrs. Grundy. Prudery has taken the spontaneity from life. Dancing is forbidden, men may not use the words *mare, bull,* or *stallion* in mixed company, and literature is censored. Moreover, the sturdy Saxon cowboys, now "under the fetid curse of hypocrisy," as McDee puts it, have physically decayed: "The slovenliness was—it's not easy to describe—it was in the whole put-together of their features, the way their noses were, and the absence of point in their eyes, and the want of accent in their mouths and chins. A total slackness. As if they were wax that had been too near the fire and had run slightly, and it had melted the meaning out of whatever mouths and noses they started with. Any good dog or horse has a neater, more personal expression."[11]

On a ranch Doc Leonard meets Mrs. Maxon, a dreadful hypocrite who curses her children like a longshoreman when she thinks no one can overhear, but who bristles with righteous indignation when it is

suggested that her weekly square dancing is "dancing," a sin; in her
mind the "skip to my Lou" chorus which accompanies the steps
makes it "singing," which is acceptable.

Later, in town, Doc Leonard runs into her husband and realizes
that the man is arranging with a black pimp for an assignation in a
whorehouse. The luckless pimp accidentally sets Mr. Maxon up with
his own wife, who it seems is given to moonlighting as a whore for
excitement when her husband is away. In a rage, Maxon kills the
pimp and drags his wife back to the ranch. When Doc Leonard sees
them the next day, both act as if nothing has happened.

The longest, and finest, story in *When West Was West* is "The
Right Honorable the Strawberries," the best fiction that Wister wrote
in the last thirty years of his life. The main character is a fictionalization of that English lord-cum-cowboy that Wister created in the
early 1890s in "The Evolution of the Cowboy," in which he argued
that the American cowboy was a modern avatar of the medieval Saxon
knight and racially and emotionally akin to British nobility. In
"Strawberries," a mysterious young English nobleman appears on the
plains of Wyoming. His full name is too unwieldy for the locals who,
discovering that his family crest pictures strawberries, call him "The
Right Honorable the Strawberries," immediately shortened to
"Strawberries." After initial awkwardness, Strawberries flourishes on
the rough frontier, winning the trust and friendship of the cowboys
by his Saxon virtues—bravery, straight shooting, physical grace, ability to hold his liquor, and a manly way with women. He is soon one
of the boys, if an odd one, although only the ubiquitous Wisterian
alter ego, the narrator, can appreciate his true mettle, and the subtlety of his aristocratic taste and lineage.

Despite his successful adaptation to western life, it is soon evident
that Strawberries is an outcast from his native England and that a
cloud hangs over his past. Still, he thrives for years, until one day
another English lord visits Wyoming, a former friend and school-
mate. Strawberries evidently hopes that his old friend will bring word
that he has been forgiven, but the newcomer snubs him, indicating
that the exile is permanent. Strawberries goes into an abrupt decline
and takes up compulsive gambling, which had apparently caused his
previous downfall. With self-respect gone, his moral character de-
cays, and he takes to cheating at cards. A small band of card sharks,
who have always resented his noble mien, plot to kill him. Strawberries is saved only through the intervention of his lowly, loyal cowboy

pal, Chalkeye, who dies rescuing his British idol with feet of clay. In an epilogue, the narrator returns by motorcar in 1910 to the town of Drybone, a sentimental journey to the scene of the action many years before. To his astonishment, he finds Strawberries living in the ghost town, decrepit, unhealthy, and totally decayed, yet still retaining an echo of the grace and nobility he once projected. Like Lord Jim, he is serving a self-imposed penance in the wilderness.

Wister touches many of the thematic bases of his Western fiction in "Strawberries." He paints western society vividly, both in its heyday and its decline in the story. He explores the opposition between "quality" and "equality," pursues the concept of the chivalric cowboy to an uncompromising conclusion, and presents the "new" West as a land of shattered illusions where a vibrant life-style has turned sour and given way to a trashy society.

The last entry in *When West Was West*, "At the Sign of the Last Chance," is less a story than a singularly appropriate epilogue to Owen Wister's Western writing. The protagonists are his cowboys, grown old. "The decline of their day began possibly with the first wire fence; the great ranch life was hastened to its death by the winter snows of 1886; received its mortal stroke in the rustler war of 1892; breathed its last—no it was still breathing, it had not wholly given up the ghost."[12] The talk of the old men muttering about the days of old in a rundown bar has a tonal rather than a narrative quality. Their fragmented stories and half-forgotten tales mingle with their grumbling laments to create an overpoweringly melancholy atmosphere. As Richard Etulain notes, "This yarn centers on feeling and mood rather than on character and conflict of values."[13] All the sound and fury, the physical and moral battles, of the early West have simmered down to this dying fall. The promise of the future, so strong in Wister's early stories through *The Virginian*, has given way completely to brooding on an unrealized past. The healthy "barbaric yawp" of Lin McLean and his friends has yielded to ancestral voices, not prophesying but pathetically recollecting. Like the barflies of O'Neill's *The Iceman Cometh*, these men live in a halting re-creation of the past, avoiding the present and the future. And like O'Neill's derelicts at Harry Hope's saloon, they pull themselves together for one last symbolic confrontation with reality. They, and the narrator, are aware that in burying the saloon's sign they are burying their lives. They can no longer even remember the stories they have told endlessly of the past. They and their world are gone. All that is left is the written record, the legacy of a few men like Wister who saw the West when it "was West" and wrote it down.

Wister left the account of what the West had been in his early fiction. In *When West Was West* he recorded what it had become. Overall the stories of the collection are surprisingly strong. We need to go back more than thirty years to the 1896 publication of *Red Men and White* to find Wister producing as uniformly excellent a gathering. There is a consistency of vision in these stories that adds greatly to the richness of description and incident that Wister brought forward from his earlier work. There is depth of character development, too, and a heightened complexity of philosophic exploration here that transcends many of the trick twists of plot and grotesqueries of character that flawed *The Jimmyjohn Boss* and *Members of the Family*. Even the two tales with melodramatic, unconvincing endings, "Bad Medicine" and "Lone Fountain," make up in characterization what they lose in narrative resolution.

It is overall seriousness of theme, however, that raises *When West Was West* above the level of Wister's earlier collections. In each story, there is a moving portrait of fallen greatness. The greatness is that of the early West which Wister had seen and presented in his first fiction as a world of almost infinite potential and an essential moral and spiritual health. But the West that appears in these stories is a fifth-act tragic hero. This world has sold its soul to the same type of "Replacers" who Wister wrote of as destroying the South in *Lady Baltimore*. Still, a sense of its former promise and splendor lingers, embodied in the over-the-hill heroes who struggle through these tales. Doc Leonard, Colonel Steptoe McDee, and even the aging "Strawberries" retain much of the dignity and spirit that marked the great days—the 1880s and early 1890s when Lin McLean and the Virginian and Scipio Le Moyne found in Wyoming a field where manhood could thrive and approach nobility.

More than anything else Wister wrote, *When West Was West* projects a genuine tragic vision in the artistic sense. In delineating believably the greatness of the loss in the failure of the western dream, *When West Was West* approaches what James Folsom in his excellent little book *The American Western Novel* sees as the potential greatness of Western writing:

In any case, the theme of the civilizing of the Great West and of the passing of the frontier, metaphorically identified in Western literature with the passing of youth, becomes a vehicle for the exploration of the ironies inherent in human endeavor. Of all these ironies, the greatest is the cherished human notion of the possibility of a new start, of another golden age more closely modeled on the land of the heart's desire. But every beginning implies an end, and here is the tragic vision of the literature of the Great West; for a golden age seems precious only after it has been lost, and the beauty of youth may only be understood from the perspective of age.[14]

Chapter Seven
Lady Baltimore

When Wister turned away from the West for the writing of *Lady Baltimore* he had established himself as the most successful Western writer in America. *The Virginian* had been the best-selling American novel of 1902 and 1903, and if its sales had leveled off, the public's enthusiasm for the novel continued in the years following its publication.[1] And *The Virginian* was only the capstone of a whole body of tales about Lin McLean, Specimen Jones, Scipio Le Moyne, and other uneducated and uncultivated "characters" who acted out these quaint tales in barroom brawls, Indian fights, and mining camp poker games. Through the 1890s and the first half-decade of the twentieth century, Wister had staked out his claim as the creator of a local-color world not very different from that of Bret Harte. His public was little ready for *Lady Baltimore*.

The book was published in 1906, a languid Jamesian novel of a well-bred northerner's discovery of true aristocracy in turn-of-the-century Charleston. For readers expecting again the broad sweep of the plains, folksy slang, and the constant promise of violence, Wister offered an extended sketch of the South's most deliberately civilized city, a novel of manners with little plot but much discussion of the virtues of grace and propriety. Although *Lady Baltimore* was well-received critically,[2] reviewers did not contain their surprise at the studied elegance of Wister's subject, "real society," and they unanimously pointed out the singularity of such a work coming from the author of *The Virginian*. The general public was obviously disappointed, and after modest sales in 1906, *Lady Baltimore* lapsed into critical and popular obscurity, seldom mentioned and more seldom read.

The neglect is doubly unfortunate. First, the enormous impact of *The Virginian* on the development of American literary and popular mythology should dictate consideration of Wister's only other novel-length fiction (and *Lin McLean*, after all, treads a thin line between being a novel and a gathering of related tales). But even discounting the importance of *The Virginian, Lady Baltimore* is an interesting book in its own right—well written in sections and fascinating in its presentation of a social philosophy designed to raise the hackles of any American not born to membership in the Union League, as Wister was.

Even solely as a one-sided and adulatory portrait of Charleston—Kings Port in *Lady Baltimore,* as thinly disguised as Thomas Wolfe's "Pulpit Hill"—the novel is impressive. Jay Hubbell believed that the work shows keener insight into southern life than any other novel written by a northerner, and that Wister captures the sense of place with a skill approaching that of George Meredith and Henry James.[3] Through the sensibility of the narrator, Augustus, Wister sketches the city with the perception of a romantic but observant devotee:

Thus it was that I came to sojourn in the most appealing, the most lovely, the most wistful town in America; whose visible sadness and distinction seem also to speak audibly, speak in the sound of the quiet waves that ripple round her Southern front, speak in the church-bells on Sunday morning, and breathe not only in the soft salt air, but in the perfume of every gentle, old-fashioned rose that blooms behind the high garden walls of falling mellow-tinted plaster: Kings Port the retrospective, Kings Port the belated, who from her pensive porticoes looks over her two rivers to the marshes and the trees beyond, the live-oaks, veiled in gray moss, brooding with memories! Were she my city, how I should love her![4]

Romantic as the passage is, it indicates that Wister's vision of Charleston is not without the specificity of realism. If, as Carl Bode claims, *The Virginian* is the kind of book "James should have shuddered at,"[5] *Lady Baltimore* is a novel he should have warmed to as an addition to the literature of aesthetic sensibility projected through objective detail. Like Howells's and James's travel writing, *Lady Baltimore* is chock-full of the concrete specifics of the Charlestonian scene, supplemented in the 1905 Hurst & Co. edition by dozens of sketches of Charleston itself by Vernon Howe Bailey. The captions of these sketches, taken from the body of Wister's text, are an index to the novel's rich and exact portrait of an antique town, its every artifact an embodiment of decaying gentility and preserved tradition: "Up the silent walks to the silent verandas"; "Leafy enclosures dipping below sight among quaint and huddled quadrangles"; "As cracks will run through fine porcelain so do these black rifts of Africa [the black sections of the city] lurk almost invisible among the gardens." The tone is that of an awed romantic, but the eye is that of James, Wharton, or Howells.

Although the physical and geographical picture of Kings Port is extensive in *Lady Baltimore,* the true subject of the novel is the absolute gentility of old Charleston as set against the tastelessness of new Charleston, and worse, northern riffraff (the deferential and apologetic narrator, Augustus, excepted). The old society of Kings Port is against everything "new" and "ill-bred," and the two terms are tautologically interchangeable. In *Lady Baltimore,* "new" and "ill-bred" applies to most of the dominant forces in turn-of-the-century America: the stock market, universal suffrage, and "the immigrant sewage of Europe." As old Charleston sees it, America has sold out on the one hand to Mammon and on the other to the canaille, both embodied in the "yellow rich" social climbers, the parvenues who lure into their bower of bliss, newly "fashionable," nouveau rich Newport, Rhode Island, what remnants of true breeding may be left in the nation. Wister calls these nouveau riche the "Replacers." They are all of a type—bankers, philanthropists, and women who smoke; "a banker," says Augustus, "is merely an ace in the same pack where a drummer is a two-spot."

In contrast to the Replacers, Wister sets the old Charleston gentry, or what is left of it forty years after the Civil War. These lingering and impoverished aristocrats are, to Wister, "the last of their kind, the end of the chain, the bold original stock, the great race that made our glory grow . . . the good old native blood of independence." In *Lady Baltimore,* they are mainly old women, like Mrs. Weguelin St. Michael, who believes that "good taste should be a sort of religion." Wister is unequivocally on their side, the side of the angels, and Augustus says, "The St. Michaels and the Replacers will never meet in this world, and I see no reason why they should in the next." Much of the novel consists of a doleful lament for "what American refinement once was, the manners we've lost, the decencies we've banished, the standards we've lowered."

Once Wister has established this tension between the old and the new, his thin plot proceeds predictably. The Replacers, led by a northern first-generation-rich industrial heiress named Hortense, descend upon Kings Port like a plague of vermin, running over the heroine's beloved dog, defiling old landmarks with cigarette butts, and talking business in churches whose walls are lined with plaques to the memory of the glorious dead. Hortense's intuition, not to mention her style, is a cut above that of the rich rabble with whom she moves, and she is determined to marry John Mayrant, the only young male representative of old Charleston in the novel. Mrs. Weguelin St. Michael and all that is decent in Kings Port are opposed. Besides instinctively despising Hortense and her "crowd," the old ladies have their own candidate for Mayrant's affections—Eliza La Heu, a local girl of good family, too reserved to show her interest in Mayrant and too proud to compete with the vulgar Hortense. When we take up the story, Mayrant has already become afianced in haste and is repenting at leisure. He realizes his folly in slumming but, caught upon a point of honor, wonders if he can break the engagement. He struggles with his conscience, decides he can back out the day before the wedding, and does. The Replacers leave and Kings Port is victorious. The town returns to the well-bred stagnation that Wister pictured at the beginning of *Lady Baltimore*. The life of the city is to be aristocratically static and uninterrupted. The rest is silence.

If Wister's locale in *Lady Baltimore* is a radical departure from that of his Westerns, his narrative approach is not. Again the story is told by Wister's now-familiar peripatetic alter ego, this time a traveler in an antique land rather than a raw, new one. Still, the narrator of this novel is basically unchanged from that of the Western stories—the curious and deferential stranger, fascinated and enchanted by an alien but appealing world that he finds increasingly sympathetic to his most fundamental feelings and beliefs. In *Lady Baltimore* the narrator is even closer to the real Wister than in *The Virginian,* for in actuality Wister never was either as proficient in western skills nor as involved in violent dramatic action as the narrator of the Western stories. But the urbane, diffident northern professional man of good manners and no pressing vocation, alternately bemused and entranced by Charleston gentility and always simpatico in the eyes of the old aristocrats—that man is Wister so thoroughly that only technical accuracy should keep us from identifying the narrator with his creator.

Whether we consider the narrator as Wister himself or a persona, what is remarkable about *Lady Baltimore* is an unabashed homage to aristocratic tradition and class distinction. Even taking into account the shift in social perspective between our time and 1905, the novel is exceptionally virulent in its attack on the principles of democracy, and nowhere is this so evident as in Wister's discussions of race. "I often think," says Augustus, "that if we could only deport the negroes [*sic*] and Newport together to one of our distant islands, how happily our two chief problems would be solved." The remark is typical of the novel, in which Wister also expresses his opinion that "Africans" with the vote are morally inferior to those without it and to their slave parents and that lynching is objectionable only on aesthetic grounds. At one point Augustus indignantly declares, "Had I a son . . . I would sooner witness him starve than hear him take orders from a menial race." Finally, the reader is treated to a scene in which it is pointed out that the Negroid and Caucasian skulls differ radically, and each difference is one in which the Negroid is more like that of the ape.

Racism had been simmering in Wister's writing for a long time before it came to a boil in *Lady Baltimore*. From the earliest stories, Wister's work is sprinkled with racial stereotypes—"deceitful" and "greasy" Mexicans, "childlike" and "primitive" Indians, and the "taint" of "Baron Hirsh," Wister's caricature of the Jewish banker. That hauteur and "difficulty" with "inferiors" that Fanny Kemble noted in her daughter, Sarah Butler Wister, developed intense racial overtones in her grandson's attitudes. But *Lady Baltimore* represents such a sudden, virulent, and unexpected outpouring of distaste for blacks and Jews as to invite some comment. Interestingly, nothing in the Wister family papers or in Wister's other writings indicates any reason why Owen Wister should have either intensified his prejudices during the writing of this novel or felt a need to air them publically. In fact, Wister's published writings tend to be more racist than his private correspondence.

He had been feeling for years, of course, increasingly sympathetic toward the South, and even at the turn of the century, the single issue that still divided southern aristocracy from northern was that of racial attitudes. The "good" families of Philadelphia, New York, and Boston might have felt socially, aesthetically, and emotionally akin to the "good" families of Richmond, Savannah, and Charleston, but the Wetherills of Philadelphia, the Jays of New York, the Lowells of Boston were part of a large northern aristocracy whose forebears had taken their abolition seriously. And even at the turn of the century, Charleston was still the city that had literally driven out the socially prominent Grimké sisters before the Civil War for suggesting that the black race might not be inferior.[6] No amount of good breeding could make up for the "wrong" attitude on the race issue, and no northerner could be truly admitted to Charleston society who did not at least tacitly accept the doctrine of Negro inferiority. Perhaps Wister, drawn powerfully to the social aesthetics of Charleston life, bent over backwards to adopt the town's social biases as well. Whatever pressures compelled Wister, *Lady Baltimore* represents an unabashed outpouring of racist attitudes unmatched in the fiction of any other major American writer of the twentieth century.

The other persistent theme, along with class consciousness, that informs *Lady Baltimore* is patriotism. If not as unpopular in critical circles as racism, it is hardly likely to win the novel many admirers today. As Wister sees it, America is sick (largely because of a decreasing number of Anglo-Saxons, no doubt), but still "young and vigorous." He pleads for unity, particularly of North and South. "There's nothing united about these States anymore except Standard Oil and discontent," Augustus complains. When asked what he wants to be, he says, "Not a Northerner nor a Southerner—an American." This aspect of Wister's social philosophy is surely more attractive than his views on class and race and perhaps easier to understand today than his respect for formalities and conventions which the Charlestonians of *Lady Baltimore* "tread like a polished French floor." This concern for national unity also foreshadowed the next stage of Wister's writing career during and after World War I, when he turned from fiction to the writing of philosophical and political tracts that were in no small part appeals to Americans to resolve internal differences and accept a commonality of interest in the face of external threats. Thus, although *Lady Baltimore* is on the one hand the most belligerently regional of Wister's local-color fiction, it is the one that most dramatically rejects sectionalism, particularly in terms of promoting one area of the country at the expense of others.

This is the world of *Lady Baltimore*—haughty, urbane, aristocratic, projecting a code of strict social and racial hierarchy and celebrating the value of tradition. There seems at first glance little in Kings Port that squares with the world of Wister the author of the archetypal Western. Superficially the novel has, beyond specificity of place, few of the basic characteristics of the Western and Southwestern Humor branches of the Local Color movement from which most of Wister's fiction seems to come. In *Lady Baltimore* Wister appears to hold up Charleston as a shining image of gentility in almost deliberate contrast to the wild egalitarianism of Harte, Bierce, and more significantly, Mark Twain. For Twain, Wister's mistily romantic Charleston with its "brittle old letters spotted with tears / and a wound that ran-

kles for fifty years" would have smacked of that "Sir Walter Scottism"
that Twain blasted in *Life on the Mississippi* and other polemics against
southern romanticism.

But *Lady Baltimore* is not simply an anomalous exotic bloom
among the sturdy cottonwoods of the Western fiction of Wister. It
was written out of the same impulse that produced *The Virginian* and
Wister's shorter tales, and it reflects more truly and obviously the author's attitude toward American society in the Gilded Age. South
Carolina and Wyoming were both appealing to Wister in their mutual distance from New York, and it was largely because he saw both
as areas in which societal hierarchy still existed in defiance of the lev-
eling influences transforming the Northeast. In Charleston, an en-
trenched aristocracy grounded its claim to social superiority in
tradition. In the West, as Wister saw it, something akin to a racist
version of Jefferson's Natural Aristocracy[7] worked itself out in rough
fashion to produce a rude social structure in which the Anglo-Saxon
cream (always called Saxons by Wister) naturally rose.

We have already seen that Wister's West was pervaded by an attitude toward man and society that sets the author apart from Twain
and Harte. Unlike them, Wister does not really give the reader a
cross section of a heterogeneous society of colorful characters. Like
Kings Port of *Lady Baltimore*, Wister's West is a solidly structured
world in which there is a sharp dichotomy between the good people
and the bad. Because the western picture is painted in more gaudy
colors than the southern one, we at first perhaps don't notice the crucial split between the elect and the damned. The Virginian, Specimen Jones, Governor Ballard, Powhattan Wingo, and Colonel
Steptoe McDee are a bit more obviously eccentric than Mrs. Weguelin St. Michael and her fellow dinosaurs, but that is perhaps only because the western setting elicits and emphasizes oddity of character.
Like the old ladies, however, the western heroes are all among the
elect because of qualities they do not have. They are not cheap, venal,
and common, as the Replacers of *Lady Baltimore* are.

Nor are they representative of the mass of humanity. As in *Lady
Baltimore*, Wister's picture of social determinism is strongly racist and
authoritarian. The Virginian, Lin McLean, Specimen Jones, and the
stout cowboys of the town of Drybone can be softened and refined by
the discipline of civilization only because they are of solid, white,
English stock like the ladies of Kings Port. Wister's version of the
West is obviously the product of the same author who wrote *Lady*

Baltimore as a reverent homage to Charleston society. In both cases, it is a picture of a shoddy and chaotic world through which move the calming representatives of culture and order,[8] spreading their steadying influence like oil on troubled and dirty waters. That the forces of order are invariably "Saxon" is only a reflection of a belief in "the white man's burden" that Wister shared with much of the Victorian world. The heroes of Wister's cowboy fiction are essentially versions of the "genuine" aristocracy the author saw in Charleston, and the villains are simply the Replacers and the "trash," black and white, of that city in a western landscape. The real world and social attitudes of Owen Wister are reflected in the Charleston of *Lady Baltimore;* the characters of his better-known Western tales are only the characters of that society in action in an exotic setting.

Chapter Eight

Summary

We may look at Owen Wister's writing now with the perspective of half a century, but it is still difficult to categorize him. In part this is because the success of *The Virginian* forces us to consider Wister as a cultural phenomenon rather than as an artist. Mainly, though, Wister's artistic diversity defies the labeling process dear to literary critics.

Most arguably he is a slightly belated entrant in the Local Color school. The strongest force in his writing is the impulse to define a piece of America, and he is therefore characteristic of American writers in the Gilded Age. As Carlos Baker points out, "The regionalist impulse in one form or another accounted for the emergence of almost every prominent writer in the Middle Atlantic States . . . in the last quarter of the century."[1] As a writer of the West, he is the successor of Harte, Joaquin Miller, Ambrose Bierce, and Mark Twain—men who introduced the reading public to the America beyond the Mississippi and the Middle Border. His works consistently exhibit the two essential characteristics of true regional literature: a concern for establishing the concrete and objective facts of the regional world, and motivation of action that arises primarily from that world's particularity.

The concern with objective particulars, of course, suggests that Wister was a Realist, and certainly there are strong realistic elements in his art. He was almost obsessive about the verisimilitude of his fictional West. He extended the material in his meticulous journals, scrupulously verifying distances against train schedules, questioning informants on specificity of detail, and reading deeply in western history. Beyond re-creating mere photographic accuracy, he took pride in presenting the frontier unsentimentally, without the dewy glow of incident and rhetoric that suffused Ned Buntline's dime novels and would soon taint the work of Zane Gray.[2] He is generally uncompromising in his choice of subject, evenhandly offering the good with the bad, the outstanding and the banal of the western experience. He can describe a Wyoming valley as a garden of Eden, or sketch a West Texas town less appetizing than Tobacco Road. Wild Goose Jake of "The Promised Land," who is not so much romantically evil as just personally and morally ugly, is as representative of Wister's characters as the Virginian. Wister gives us "the old days, the happy days, when Wyoming was a Territory with a future instead of a State with a past," but he also gives us the philistine world of "Padre Ignazio."

So grim, in fact, is much of his world, and so deterministic the fates of many of his characters, that Wister's realism often borders on Naturalism. This is particularly true in the later stories collected in *Members of the Family* and *When West Was West*—stories of men overtaken by time, defeated by circumstance, and waging the good fight in a world where man is a wolf unto man. But the stories of the 1890s, too, often reveal a concern with the implacable force of nature and the theme of man as a functioning animal, struggling to survive in a hostile environment.

Further, the deceptive assumption that a true naturalist's sympathies must lie with victims may keep many readers from recognizing that Wister's social vision is similar to Dreiser's. Wister's society, with constant class war between the "quality" and the "equality," has overtones of social Darwinism, as do the racial presuppositions that underlie his constant presentation of Saxons as "naturally" superior to other racial groups.[4] Wister's social world, like his natural one, is often "red in tooth and claw," a competitive society in which the fittest survive or prevail. Not the least of the sins of characters like Shorty in *The Virginian,* Horacles in "Happy-Teeth," or Dr. Salamanca in the Texas stories is a failure to realize their natural inferiority.

Still, it is hard to see Wister as a Naturalist. In part, this is because personally and in his art he rejected all the forces that produced Naturalism—new money, competitive capitalism, immigration, social mobility, industrialization, populism, conspicuous consumption, pragmatism, and behaviorism. Also, where the Naturalists display a studied moral objectivity, Wister is constantly passing judgment.

In many respects we might most comfortably consider Wister a romantic. His original subtitle for *The Virginian* was "A Romance," and through story after story his narrator avowedly pursues an idealism that he often fails to find, wearing his cavalier heart on his sleeve. In "The Evolution of the Cowboy," he limned a prototype for fiction straight out of Arthurian legendry. Stylistically, his frequent lapses into elevated rhetoric—poetic in attempt, bombastic in effect—are complemented by frequent reliance on what Howells called "the blue-fire of melodrama." The Virginian's dramatic rescue of Molly from the runaway stage, Lin McLean's cloying adoption of the biscuit shooter's cast-off son, and the apparition of the god Apollo in "Lone Fountain" would all have appalled James, who handled apparitions more delicately. Sentimentality drips from the worst of Wister's scenes, and when he has difficulty developing a progress naturally he too often falls back on the long arm of coincidence, accompanied by spontaneous overflow of emotion. What, after all, are the chances that Molly will be the one to find the Virginian after the Indians wound him?

Whether a Realist, a Naturalist, or a romantic, Wister was consistently one thing—a writer of the fiction of manners, in his case the regional manners of the West. His leitmotif is the character of western society. As James Tuttleton writes in *The Novel of Manners in America*, "America has always had those variegated customs, that complexity of manners and types, that hum and buzz of implication, which forms a fund of suggestion for our writers."[5] Wister's *donnée* was the "hum and buzz" of the West. He recorded it as truly as possible and suggested through dramatic action some of the resultant implications.

That society as Wister pictures it is rich and various. As with most Local Color writers, characterization was a strong point with him, and some of his most effective creations were "Characters" with a capital C to rival the eccentrics of Harte, Twain, or Cable. One character that Wister virtually invented was the "dude." This is inevitably a good-hearted but inept easterner, usually the narrator, wandering wide-eyed in the strange, rough western world. The dude was of course modeled on Wister himself, and it is through him that we see the rest of the cast. This callow tyro counterpoints the virtues of the cowboy hero—idealized virtues in the case of the Virginian, but virtues balanced by believable weaknesses in diamonds in the rough like Specimen Jones and Scipio Le Moyne.

Wister's villains are perhaps more vivid than his heroes. The blatant malevolence of Trampas is actually a rare unequivocal characterization in Wister's rogues' gallery. Not so with the "drummer," a persistent character who frequently crosses the line from noisome venality to outright villainy. Shifty, loud-mouthed, overly familiar, and manipulative, Wister's drummers, salesmen, peddlers, and promoters spoil the potential purity of the West. Yet not all are equally loathsome—the Manna Baby Food salesman in "Twenty Minutes for Refreshments" is more a colorful, windy Barnum that a villain, and Uncle Pasco has a sense of humor that mitigates his evil. Often Wister's badmen are less vicious than just victims of their own mindless violence. The cowboy gang in "The Jimmyjohn Boss," Drylyn in "Salvation Gap," and the rebellious ex-Confederates of "The Second Missouri Compromise" are men in whom spirit runs dangerously higher than their reason can control.

Whether "good guys" or "bad guys," Wister's people are generally believable. Occasionally their idiosyncrasies seem a trifle contrived—like the otherwise plebeian Specimen Jones's constant singing of Elizabethan madrigals and songs in German—but for the most part Wister's characters fit into a convincing fictional society, which is composed of all sorts and conditions of men and has, understandably, a disproportionate share of the strange, the colorful, and the grotesque. Many of these eccentrics are compelling creations: Max Vogel, the German-American cattle boss; Powhatten Wingo, the florid ex-Confederate legislator, and Mrs. Porcher Brewton, the bustling, peripatetic grande dame of "Twenty Minutes for Refreshments."

If Wister's command of style and structure in these writings had been equal to his gift for characterization and his eye for social nuance and detail, he might have produced some truly substantial contributions to literature. Unfortunately, they were not. Wister shifts stylistically from powerful reporting to tendentious and rambling pontificating. Dialogue is similarly uneven, alternating between clean, believable conversation and colorful westernisms and awkward clots of euphuistic philosophizing. Considering how well he *could* write, it is a shame he didn't write better—and more.

Which is not to say that Wister does not have a legitimate place in American literary history, and an important one. He is still the very best writer to deal with an important aspect of the nation's experience. His eye and ear were keener than those of any other writer fictionalizing the West. Twain would have been better, but he left only *Roughing It* and retreated to the Mississippi Valley for his main theme. Bierce was a better technician than Wister, a more skillful manipulator of plot with a more powerful sense of the truly dramatic and a deeper understanding of psychology, but Bierce was only nominally a Western writer. Harte left four or five good stories—none of them as carefully observed as the best of Wister—and then rehashed them endlessly. Wister, though, left a considerable body of substantial fiction, re-creating a western world in depth and with scope. Oregon, Wyoming, Texas, Arizona—his fiction covered a wide and varied landscape. Cowboys, Indians, soldiers, drummers, drunks, bishops, and medicine men: a rich dramatis personae. If his dramatic development sometimes falters, it as often moves convincingly, often movingly, to resolution. He was, as he claimed, an artist rather than simply a Western writer.

Even were it not, then, for the enormous impact of *The Virginian,* Wister should still be read, although he seldom is. Still, though, when we consider what he was capable of, we wonder why he was not a greater writer. He had a vision of the American West as the last fair field upon which could be tested the morality and culture of Western civilization. But he never explored the vision, or probed it to its depths, or worked it out in a major work. And too often he fell back on cheap rhetoric and jejeune structuring rather than working for the hard craftsmanship that would have bodied forth his vision with convincing substance. Why will Wister always be regarded as a minor regional writer instead of producing the great novel of the West which has never been written?

One answer is that it was a failure of Wister's times rather than of the man himself. Surely the period in which he worked was an unfelicitous one for American literature. As Larzer Ziff says of the decade after the publication of *The Virginian,* when Wister's "great" work should have come, "The years from 1902 to 1912 form the single most dreary decade in the nation's letters." As a sympathetic critic suggests of Wister, "Why did he not write better? Certainly one of the reasons, if not the only one, was the temper of the times."[7] Yet some writers overcame "the temper of the times," for James and Howells and the naturalists produced major work during this period.

Perhaps the answer lies in Wister's life and world. He may, indeed, have been "Philadelphia's last distinguished gentleman of letters,"[8] but he may also have been the product of a world in which a gentleman could be a "distinguished" writer, but not a great one. Wister himself wrote of Philadelphians, "We seem to distrust our own power to do anything out of the common; and when a young man tries to, our minds close against him with a civic instinct of disparagement. A Boston failure in art surprises Boston; it is success that surprises Philadelphia."[9] Wister may have recognized the aristocratic distrust of creativity, but he could not escape from it. Unlike

Edith Wharton, he could not bring himself to turn his back on his class, and so he carried its prejudices and its fundamental shallowness into his fiction. He took something more debilitating, too—a fundamental lack of commitment to writing. Wister cared about literature—far more than other members of his class—but in the final analysis it was more important to him to function as a gentleman within his aristocrat world.

The western experience, and the literary career that for Wister became inextricably bound up in that experience, always remained for him what it had been during that summer of 1885 when he got off the train in Wyoming and found a world more exciting and beautiful than anything he had ever imagined—and more alien. He tried very hard to render the West in literature, and he was not unsuccessful. But the great and definitive statement eluded him. Just as he felt in 1885 the irreconcilable tension between his mother's mores and the West's freedom, so all his life he was pulled back from his writing into his role as a gentleman. His family, his society, his education, and ultimately his instincts combined to keep him from being the writer that he might have been. His epitaph could be taken from a letter Ernest Hemingway wrote to Max Perkins, saying of Wister, "He could have been a very great writer and the combination of circumstances that prevent that are always tragic."[10]

Notes and References

Chapter One

1. Alexander Woollcott, "Wisteria," *New Yorker* 6 (August 1930):30.
2. Frances Anne Kemble, *Journal of a Residence on a Georgian Plantation in 1838–1839,* ed. John A. Scott (New York, 1961).
3. The Butler-Kemble divorce was an unusually unpleasant one, even by modern standards. Papers and letters relevant to the action, along with a lengthy attack on Fanny Kemble circulated by Pierce Butler among his friends, can be found with the Wister papers in the archives of the Philadelphia Historical Society.
4. G. Edward White, *The Eastern Establishment and the Western Experience: The West of Frederic Remington, Theodore Roosevelt, and Owen Wister* (New Haven, 1968), p. 68.
5. From Fanny Kemble's *Memoirs,* quoted in White, *The Eastern Establishment,* p. 68.
6. The Wister letters in the Philadelphia Historical Society are full of references by Sarah Butler Wister concerning her inability to find servants and by her husband, Owen Jones Wister, on her inability to keep them.
7. Henry James, quoted in Fanny Kemble Wister, *That I May Tell You* (Wayne, 1979), p. 8.
8. Fanny Kemble Wister, *Owen Wister Out West: His Journals and Letters* (Chicago, 1958), p. 23.
9. George Thomas Watkins, III, "Owen Wister and the American West: A Biographical and Critical Study." Ph.D. diss., University of Illinois, 1959, p. 23.
10. John Lukacs, "Owen Wister," *American Heritage,* March 1981, p. 57.
11. Owen Wister to Sarah Butler Wister, quoted in Frances Kemble Wister Stokes, *My Father, Owen Wister, and Ten Letters Written by Owen Wister to His Mother during his First Trip to Wyoming in 1885* (Laramie: University of Wyoming Library Association, 1952), p. 6.
12. Ibid., p. 3.
13. White, *The Eastern Establishment,* p. 69.
14. Leon Edel, *The Conquest of London: 1870–1881,* Vol. 2 of *Henry James* (New York: J.B. Lippincott, 1962; New York: Avon, 1968), p. 108.
15. Watkins, "Wister and the American West," p. 23. Watkins's dissertation is by far the best single source of information on Dr. Owen Jones Wister.

16. Julian Mason, "Owen Wister, Boy Librarian," *Quarterly Journal of the Library of Congress* 26 (October 1969):201.

17. Richard W. Etulain, *Owen Wister,* Boise State College Western Writers Series, no. 7 (Boise, 1973), p. 7.

18. Owen Wister, *Roosevelt: The Story of a Friendship* (New York, 1930), p. 9.

19. Ibid., p. 22.

20. Ibid., p. 22.

21. Ibid., p. 24.

22. Roosevelt's prudery is a puzzling aspect of a man who, for a politician, was uncommonly academic, intellectual, and artistic. In 1890, when the U.S. Post Office banned Tolstoy's *The Kreutzer Sonata,* Roosevelt referred to the Russian author as a "sexual and moral pervert" (Randy F. Nelson, *The Almanac of American Letters* [Los Altos, Calif.: William Kaufmann, 1981], p. 144).

23. Owen Wister, *Roosevelt,* p. 17.

24. Watkins, "Wister and the American West," p. 160.

25. Sarah Butler Wister quoted by Frances Kemble Wister, *That I May Tell You: Journals and Letters of the Owen Wister Family* (Wayne, Pa., 1979), p. 15.

26. Watkins, "Wister and the American West," p. 226.

27. Ibid., p. 271.

28. Fanny Kemble Wister, *That I May Tell You,* p. 22.

29. Ibid., p. 22.

30. Ibid., pp. 80–84.

31. Watkins, "Wister and the American West," p. 44. Watkins says it was a nervous breakdown.

32. Ben Merchant Vorpahl, *My Dear Wister——: The Frederic Remington–Owen Wister Letters* (Palo Alto, 1972), p. 8.

33. Owen Wister, *Roosevelt,* p. 28.

34. Fanny Kemble Wister, *That I May Tell You,* p. 76.

35. There is a long letter in the Wister papers in the Philadelphia Historical Society from Dr. Wister to Elizabeth R. Fisher, 6 September 1883, describing his visit to Alcott.

36. Fanny Kemble Wister, *That I May Tell You,* p. 12.

37. Watkins, "Wister and the American West," p. 183.

38. Owen Wister, *Roosevelt,* p. 58.

39. Margaret Armstrong, *Fanny Kemble* (New York, 1938), p. 357.

40. Bernard DeVoto, *The Year of Decision: 1846* (Boston: Little, Brown & Co., 1943), p. 483.

41. Walter Prescott Webb, *The Great Plains* (Boston, 1931), p. 237.

42. White, *The Eastern Establishment,* p. 123. White discusses Wister's affinity for the association. When he first came West, and repeatedly there-

after, he stayed at the association's luxurious Cheyenne Club. In the Johnson County cattle war, Wister unequivocally supported the association, which was one of the antagonists.

43. Quoted in Fanny Kemble Wister, *Owen Wister Out West,* p. 31.

44. All quotations from *Owen Wister Out West,* pp. 29–33.

45. Quoted in Fanny Kemble Wister, *Owen Wister Out West,* p. 35.

46. White, *The Eastern Establishment,* p. 124.

47. Owen Wister, *Roosevelt,* pp. 28–29.

48. Vorpahl, *My Dear Wister,* p. 23.

49. Ibid., p. 27.

50. Fanny Kemble Wister, *That I May Tell You,* pp. 122–23. Wister wrote his father on 2 July 1887 that the doctor's last letter to him caused him "astonishment and pain."

51. Quoted in Fanny Kemble Wister, *Owen Wister Out West,* p. 60. Wister wrote in his diary, "A curse on people who carve their names at these places. . . . I hope they'll have to write their names in Hell with a red-hot pen holder."

52. Ibid., p. 96.

53. Ibid., pp. 100–110.

54. Owen Wister, *Roosevelt,* p. 29. Vorpahl in *My Dear Wister,* p. 28, claims that Wister already had several Western tales complete by the spring of 1891 and that his June 1891 trip to Wyoming was made "with the specific intention of gathering material for stories." Wister does mention to his mother in a letter of 21 June 1891 that "after awhile I shall write a great fat book about the whole thing," but there doesn't seem to be much indication that he had any specific intentions along those lines. The January/ February 1984 issue of *American West* carried Wister's unfinished and previously unpublished manuscript, "The Story of Chalkeye: A Wind River Romance." The manuscript, discovered in 1971 in an attic of the Wister house in Bryn Mawr, Pa., had a note in Wister's hand written on the title page: "This was a first essay—begun early in 1891 and never finished." This manuscript obviously suggests that Wister came to Western writing more slowly and carefully than he would have us believe in *Roosevelt: The Story of a Friendship,* and the story of the epiphany of the "sagebrush Kipling" gives way to a picture of a more conventional trial-and-error apprenticeship as a writer.

55. Owen Wister, *Roosevelt,* p. 30.

56. Fanny Kemble Wister, *Owen Wister Out West,* p. 196.

57. Owen Wister, *Roosevelt,* p. 34.

58. Philip Durham, introduction to *The Virginian* (1902; reprint ed., New York: Houghton Mifflin, 1968), p. x.

59. Vorpahl, *My Dear Wister,* p. 35.

60. Owen Wister, "The Evolution of the Cowboy," quoted in Vorpahl, *My Dear Wister,* p. 80. Vorpahl reprints the entire Wister essay.

61. Ibid., p. 80.

62. Ibid., p. 80.

63. Ibid., p. 94.

64. See *American Literary Realism* 7, no. 1 (Winter 1974):13 for a summary of critical reaction to "The Evolution of the Cowboy."

65. Owen Wister, "The Evolution of the Cowboy," in Vorpahl, *My Dear Wister*, p. 96.

66. Owen Wister, introduction to *Done in the Open* by Frederic Remington, quoted in N. Orwin Rush, *Frederic Remington and Owen Wister: The Story of a Friendship 1893–1909* (Tallahassee: Florida State University Press, 1961), p. 131.

67. William Dean Howells, *Harper's Weekly*, no. 39 (30 November 1895):1133.

68. Theodore Roosevelt, *Harper's Weekly*, no. 39 (21 December 1895), p. 1216.

69. Owen Wister, introduction to *Lin McLean*, 2d ed. (1897; reprint ed., New York: A. L. Burt Co., 1907), p. vii.

70. Fanny Kemble Wister, *That I May Tell You*, p. 21.

71. Owen Wister, *Roosevelt*, p. 57.

72. Ibid., p. 58.

73. Thelma Kimmel, "Washington's Methow Valley Inspired *The Virginian*," *Idaho Farmer*, 3 November 1955, pp. 28–29.

74. Owen Wister to Sarah Butler Wister, quoted in Vorpahl, *My Dear Wister*, p. 274.

75. See *American Literary Realism* 7, no. 1 (Winter 1974):19–21, for reactions to *The Jimmyjohn Boss*.

76. Owen Wister, *Ulysses S. Grant* (Boston, 1901), Bibliography, pp. 141–45.

77. See *American Literary Realism* 7, no. 1 (Winter 1974):22–23, for reactions to *Ulysses S. Grant*.

78. Owen Wister to Oliver Wendell Holmes, Jr., May 1902, quoted in Durham, introduction to *The Virginian*, p. xi.

79. Wister, *The Virginian*, p. 93.

80. Owen Wister to Sarah Butler Wister, 2 February 1902, quoted by Fanny Kemble Wister, *That I May Tell You*, p. 161.

Chapter Two

1. James D. Hart, *The Popular Book: A History of America's Literary Taste* (1950; reprint ed., Berkeley: University of California Press, 1963), p. 207.

2. A typical review by a realist critic appeared in the *Sewanee Review* 10 (October 1902):504–5, which called *The Virginian* "an impossible love story . . . a romance surcharged with sentimentality, psychologically uncon-

vincing, and artistically untrue. . . . By all means give the swearing, gambling, shooting, lynching, and the rest, and create atmosphere, but spare the sentimentalizing and the heroics."

3. Vorpahl, *My Dear Wister,* p. 308.

4. Carl Bode, "Henry James and Owen Wister," *American Literature* 26 (May 1954):251, points out that *The Virginian* was "just the kind of book James should have hated."

5. Owen Wister, *Roosevelt,* p. 106.

6. A number of Wister's letters to his mother indicate that he was uncomfortable in his dependence upon her. See, for example, the letter of 11 May 1898, quoted in Fanny Kemble Wister, *That I May Tell You,* p. 134.

7. Owen Wister, *Roosevelt,* p. 106.

8. Mary Channing Wister to Owen Wister, November 1903, quoted in Fanny Kemble Wister, *That I May Tell You,* p. 165.

9. Owen Wister, *Roosevelt,* p. 107.

10. Fanny Kemble Wister, *That I May Tell You,* p. 161.

11. The four most popular plays—the most frequently performed—in America at the turn of the century were melodramatic adaptations of popular literature: *Rip Van Winkle, Ten Nights in a Bar Room, In His Steps,* and *The Count of Monte Cristo.*

12. Owen Wister, *Roosevelt,* p. 106.

13. Fanny Kemble Wister, *That I May Tell You,* pp. 104–5.

14. Vorpahl, *My Dear Wister,* p. 98.

15. Fanny Kemble Wister, *That I May Tell You,* pp. 104–5. The letters of the Wister family in the Philadelphia Historical Society unequivocally indicate sickness.

16. Fanny Kemble Wister, *That I May Tell You,* p. 168.

17. John Lukacs, "From Camelot to Abilene," *American Heritage,* no. 32 (February-March 1981), p. 57.

18. Vorpahl, *My Dear Wister,* p. 324. All the information in this paragraph is from ibid., pp. 324–30.

19. Fanny Kemble Wister, *That I May Tell You,* p. 175.

20. Ibid., p. 179.

21. Vorpahl, *My Dear Wister,* p. 327.

22. Fanny Kemble Wister, *That I May Tell You,* p. 179.

23. Ibid., p. 188.

24. Ibid., p. 192. Wister also used the Lohengrin analogy describing the West in the preface to *Members of the Family.*

25. Owen Wister, *Members of the Family* (New York, 1911), p. 7.

26. Ibid., p. 9.

27. Lukacs, "Camelot," p. 60.

28. Fanny Kemble Wister, *That I May Tell You,* p. 229. Wister's letters after Molly's death dwell repeatedly upon it.

29. The last mention of the Philadelphia novel in Wister's journal or family letters was in his journal for April of 1914. (Fanny Kemble Wister, *That I May Tell You,* p. 238). This novel was tentatively titled *Monopolis,* and four completed chapters of it survive among the Wister papers in the Library of Congress. As John Lukacs says, they are "a compound of sarcasm and nostalgia, of bitterness together with an exaltation of the other aristocratic virtues." John Lukacs, *Philadelphia: Patricians and Philistines, 1900–1950* (New York, 1981), p. 255.

30. For a full study of S. Weir Mitchell, particularly with reference to his relationship with Wister, see Joseph P. Lovering, *S. Weir Mitchell* (Boston, 1971).

31. Fanny Kemble Wister, *That I May Tell You,* p. 261.

32. Ibid., p. 257.

33. Quoted in Arthur S. Link, *Woodrow Wilson and the Progressive Era* (1954; reprint ed., New York: Harper & Row, 1963), p. 176.

34. Mark Shorer, *Sinclair Lewis: An American Life* (New York: McGraw-Hill, 1961), p. 552.

35. Wister letter to Richard Harding Davis, 6 November 1902, quoted in John M. Solensten, "Richard Harding Davis, Owen Wister, and the Virginian: Unpublished Letters and a Commentary," *American Literary Realism* 5 (Spring 1972):124.

36. Ernest Hemingway to Max Perkins, 24 June 1929, quoted in *Ernest Hemingway: Selected Letters, 1917–1961,* ed. Carlos Baker (New York: Scribner's, 1981), p. 299.

37. Ernest Hemingway to Barklie McKee Henry, 15 August 1927, quoted in ibid., p. 255.

38. Ernest Hemingway to Harvey Breit, 3 July 1956, quoted in ibid., p. 862.

39. Shorer, *Lewis,* p. 605.

40. Ernest Hemingway to Max Perkins, 15 December 1929, quoted in Baker, *Hemingway,* p. 316.

41. The most complete study of "The Right Honorable the Strawberries" is Neal Lambert, "The Values of the Frontier: Owen Wister's Final Assessment," *South Dakota Review* 9 (Spring 1971):78–87. Lambert feels that this story summarizes Wister's final attitude toward the West.

42. Charles Poore, "Owen Wister Recaptures the West," *New York Times Book Review,* 1 July 1928, p. 7.

43. Owen Wister, "Dr. Coit," *Atlantic* 142 (December 1928):756–68.

44. Owen Wister, *Roosevelt,* p. 130.

45. Ibid., p. 160.

46. Ibid., p. 256.

47. Benjamin Quarles, *The Negro in the Making of America* (1964; reprint ed., New York: MacMillan, 1969), p. 171.

48. Owen Wister, *Roosevelt,* p. 117.

49. Ibid., p. 200.

50. Fanny Kemble Wister, *That I May Tell You,* p. 217.

51. *Wilson Library Bulletin* 13 (September 1938):6.

Chapter Three

1. Etulain, *Owen Wister,* p. 32.

2. Vorpahl, *My Dear Wister,* p. 228.

3. Wister's frustrated desire to compose is often evident in his works. Many of his characters sing, and in several places in his stories, he transcribes music for description.

4. Wister, *Red Men and White* (New York, 1895), p. 81.

5. Ibid., p. 299.

6. Anonymous review, *Atlantic,* no. 77 (February 1896), pp. 264–65.

7. Philip J. Landon, review of criticism of *Red Men and White, American Literary Realism* 7, no. 1 (Winter 1974):15.

8. Vorpahl, *My Dear Wister,* p. 275.

9. Etulain, *Owen Wister,* p. 32.

10. Wister, *The Jimmyjohn Boss* (New York, 1900), p. 8.

11. Ibid., p. 63.

12. Ibid., p. 244.

13. Ibid., p. 244.

14. Ibid., p. 90.

15. Charles Olson, *Call Me Ishmael* (San Francisco: City Lights Books, 1947). This remarkable study of Melville by a major American poet opens, "I take SPACE to be the central fact to man born in America, from Folsom cave to now. I spell it large because it comes large here. Large, and without mercy" (p. 11).

16. Wister, *Red Men and White,* p. 53.

17. Ibid., p. 240.

18. Wister, *The Jimmyjohn Boss,* p. 29.

19. Ibid., p. 30.

20. Ibid., p. 193.

21. Wister, *Red Men and White,* p. 179.

22. Ibid., p. 175.

23. Ibid., p. 3.

24. Ibid., p. 5.

25. Ibid., p. 78.

26. William Dean Howells, "Life and Letters," *Harper's Weekly* no. 39 (30 November 1895):1133.

27. Wister, *Red Men and White,* p. vi.

Chapter Four

1. Vorpahl, *My Dear Wister,* pp. 168–81.
2. Wister, *Lin McLean* (1897; reprint ed., New York: A. L. Burt Co., 1907), p. vii; hereafter page references cited in the text.
3. Vorpahl, *My Dear Wister,* p. 181.
4. Fanny Kemble Wister, *Owen Wister Out West,* p. 72. Letter from Owen Wister to Sarah Butler Wister, August 1885.

Chapter Five

1. Durham, introduction to *The Virginian,* p. xiv. Durham lists the previously published stories Wister incorporated into the novel.
2. *Encyclopaedia Britannica,* 1978 ed., vol. W, p. 587.
3. James K. Folsom indulges in this cavalier interchanging of Wister himself with the anonymous narrator of *The Virginian* in a taped lecture, *The Works of Owen Wister,* Western American Writers Series, no. 1121 (Deland, Fla., 1978). Folsom's point is that the narrator is so like Wister as to invite the identification. Less responsible critics have not made even this distinction.
4. Owen Wister, *The Virginian* (1902; reprint ed., New York: Houghton Mifflin, 1968); hereafter page references cited in the text.
5. John Seelye, "When West Was Wister," *New Republic,* 2 September 1972, p. 29.
6. Letter from Owen Wister to Richard Harding Davis, 11 November 1902. Quoted in Solensten, "Richard Harding Davis, Owen Wister and the Virginian," p. 132.
7. John Williams, "The Western: Definition of the Myth." *Nation* 193 (18 November 1961):402.
8. James K. Folsom, *The American Western Novel* (New Haven, 1966), p. 113.
9. Leslie Fiedler, *The Return of the Vanishing American* (New York, 1968), pp. 138–39.
10. John K. Milton, *The Novel of the American West* (Lincoln, 1980), p. 37.
11. John G. Cawelti, *Adventure, Mystery, and Romance: Formula Stories as Art and Popular Culture* (Chicago, 1976), p. 229.

Chapter Six

1. Vorpahl, *My Dear Wister,* p. 259.
2. Ibid., p. 263.
3. Wister, *Members of the Family* (New York, 1911), p. 3.
4. Ibid., p. 187.
5. Ibid., p. iii.

6. Ibid., p. 106.

7. Ibid., p. 228.

8. Ibid., p. 20.

9. Etulain, *Owen Wister*, p. 41.

10. Wister tells us that Captain Monk was twenty-five at the time of the Lava Bed war, and then has him chasing Cochise at the age of forty. Cochise died in 1874, and the Lava Bed war ended in that year. Monk would be forty in 1889.

11. Wister, *When West Was West* (New York, 1928), p. 314.

12. Ibid., p. 414.

13. Etulain, *Owen Wister*, p. 44.

14. Folsom, *The American Western Novel*, p. 206.

Chapter Seven

1. Hart, *The Popular Book*, p. 207.

2. Literary reviews of *Lady Baltimore* were almost unanimously favorable at the time of its publication. See the *Atlantic Monthly* 99 (January 1907):99; *Book Review Digest* 2 (1906):383; *Literary Digest* 33 (August 1906):58; *Times* (London), 20 April 1906, p. 142.

3. Jay B. Hubbell, "Owen Wister's Work," *South Atlantic Quarterly* 29 (October 1930):440–43.

4. Owen Wister, *Lady Baltimore* (New York, 1906), p. 9.

5. Carl Bode, "Henry James and Owen Wister," *American Literature* 26 (May 1954):251. This is only one of several studies which point out that, although in terms of superficial realistic detail Wister owed much to James they are dissimilar in intent and technique.

6. Samuel Eliot Morison, *The Oxford History of the American People* (New York, 1965), p. 521.

7. Jefferson's attitudes on race are still a matter of controversy, but he would undoubtedly have been appalled by Wister's undemocratic version of Natural Aristocracy. As Vernon Parrington says of Jefferson, "He . . . regarded 'the better sort of people' as the chief hindrance to the spread of social justice" (Vernon L. Parrington, *The Colonial Mind; Main Currents in American Thought*, vol. 1 [1927; reprint ed., New York: Harcourt, Brace & World, 1954], p. 360).

8. I treat Wister's authoritarianism elsewhere. See also Marvin Lewis, "Owen Wister: Caste Imprints in Western Literature," *Arizona Quarterly* 10 (Summer 1954):147–56.

Chapter Eight

1. Carlos Baker, "Delineation of Life and Character," in *Literary History of the United States*, rev. ed., ed. Robert E. Spiller et al. (New York: Macmillan, 1955), p. 848.

2. Folsom, *The American Western Novel,* p. 156.

3. Wister, *Red Men and White,* p. 48.

4. Paul Witkowsky, "The Idea of Order: Frontier Societies in the Fiction of Cooper, Simms, Hawthorne, and Wister." Ph.D. diss., University of North Carolina at Chapel Hill, 1979 (DAI: 40, 3306A), p. 237.

5. James W. Tuttleton, *The Novel of Manners in America* (New York: Norton, 1972), p. 27.

6. Larzer Ziff, *The American 1890s* (New York, 1966), p. 228.

7. Walter Van Tilburg Clark, "Philadelphia Gentleman in Wyoming," *New York Times Book Review* 30 (30 March 1958):26.

8. E. Digby Baltzell, *Philadelphia Gentlemen: The Making of a National Upper Class* (Glencoe, Ill.: Free Press, 1958), p. 155

9. Owen Wister, introduction to *Bobo and Other Fancies* by Thomas Wharton (New York: Harper & Brothers, 1897), p. xiv.

10. Ernest Hemingway, letter to Max Perkins, 15 December 1929. Quoted in *Ernest Hemingway: Selected Letters,* ed. Baker, p. 316.

Selected Bibliography

Note: The two great sources for biographical information on Owen Wister are: (1) the papers of the Wister family in the Historical Society of Pennsylvania in Philadelphia, and (2) the Library of Congress. There are smaller collections of material at the University of Wyoming (including Wister's journals), the Houghton Library at Harvard, and the Beinecke Library at Yale. Students interested in the Library of Congress holdings should consult *Owen Wister: A Register of His Papers in the Library of Congress* (Washington D.C.: Library of Congress Reference Dept., Manuscript Division, 1972).

PRIMARY SOURCES

1. Novels
Lin McLean. New York: A. L. Burt, 1897.
The Virginian. New York: Macmillan, 1902.
Lady Baltimore. New York: Hurst, 1906.

2. Short Story Collections
Red Men and White. New York: Harper's, 1895.
The Jimmyjohn Boss. New York: Harper's, 1900.
Members of the Family. New York: Macmillan, 1911.
When West Was West. New York: Macmillan, 1928.

3. Major Nonfiction
Ulysses S. Grant. Boston: Small, Maynard, 1901. Biography.
The Seven Ages of Washington. New York: Macmillan, 1907. Biography.
The Pentecost of Calamity. New York: Macmillan, 1916. Political commentary.
A Straight Deal or the Ancient Grudge. New York: Macmillan, 1921. Political commentary.
Neighbors Henceforth. New York: Macmillan, 1922. Political commentary.
Roosevelt: The Story of a Friendship. New York: Macmillan, 1930. Biography and personal reminiscence.

SECONDARY SOURCES

1. Bibliographies

Marovitz, Sanford E. *Owen Wister: An Annotated Bibliography of Secondary Material. American Literary Realism: 1870–1910,* vol. 7, no. 1 (Winter 1974). By far the most comprehensive bibliographical treatment of Wister and his works to date. The starting point for all Wister scholarship. Subsumes all previous bibliographies. Complete through mid-1973.

Rush, N. Orwin. "Fifty Years of *The Virginian.*" In *The Papers of the Bibliographical Society of America* 46 (2d Quarter 1952):99–120. First major bibliography of Wister or *The Virginian.* Largely superseded by the Marovitz bibliography, but includes a sketch of the novel's background and popularity.

2. Books

Etulain, Richard W. *Owen Wister: The Western Writings.* Boise State College Western Writers Series, no. 7. Boise, Idaho: Boise State University Press. A pedestrian but useful introduction to the Western writings. Treats Wister almost entirely in terms of his importance as a chronicler of the West.

Vorpahl, Ben Merchant. *My Dear Wister—: The Frederic Remington–Owen Wister Letters.* Palo Alto: American West, 1972. The finest published work on Wister. An in-depth analysis with scrupulous scholarship on the psychologies of these two men, with particular attention to their respective arts. Most thorough for Wister for the years between 1893 and 1902. Beautifully written and structured. A minor note: sloppy index with errors and omissions.

White, G. Edward. *The Eastern Establishment and the Western Experience: The West of Frederic Remington, Theodore Roosevelt, and Owen Wister.* Yale Publications in American Studies, no. 14. New Haven: Yale University Press, 1968. A solid, scholarly treatment of the cultural implications of eastern gentry slumming on the frontier.

Wister, Fanny Kemble. *Owen Wister Out West.* Chicago: University of Chicago Press, 1958. The journals and letters of Wister's travels in the West from 1885 to the early 1890s, edited with an introduction by his daughter (Mrs. Walter Stokes) and commentary. Invaluable for tracing the roots of Wister's reactions to the West and the sources of many of the Western stories.

————. *That I May Tell You: Journals and Letters of the Owen Wister Family.* Wayne, Pa.: Haverford House, 1979. The best single published source of primary biographical information on Wister and his family. Includes

Sarah Butler Wister's Civil War journal, many letters from Wister to his mother and his wife, and Wister's personal diary, kept after his wife's death. Introductory material and commentary by Wister's daughter, Fanny Kemble Wister.

3. Parts of Books

Armstrong, Margaret. *Fanny Kemble.* New York: Macmillan, 1938. Melodramatic but accurate on Wister's influential grandmother and her impact on her family.

Branch, Douglas. *The Cowboy and His Interpreters.* New York: Cooper Square, 1961. Reprint of 1926 edition. Pages 192–200 sketch Wister's career, attack *The Virginian* for failure to depict cowboys working with cattle.

Brooks, Van Wyck. *The Confident Years: 1885–1915.* New York: Dutton, 1952. Pages 87–91 trace Wister's unusual social and academic background.

Cawelti, John G. *Adventure, Mystery, and Romance: Formula Stories as Art and Popular Culture.* Chicago: University of Chicago Press, 1976. Pages 215–30 discuss *The Virginian* in depth as pandering to the American popular fiction audience's desire for romance with the illusion of realism.

Durham, Philip, ed. Introduction to *The Virginian* by Owen Wister. Boston: Houghton Mifflin, 1968. Pages v–xii present a sketchy discussion of aspects of the novel. Good on textual information and structuring of component stories.

Fiedler, Leslie. *The Return of the Vanishing American.* New York: Stein & Day, 1968. Pages 138–39 constitute a blistering attack on Wister's authoritarianism and present him as a crypto-fascist. Provocative on "respectable" literature's treatment of the Indian.

Folsom, James K. *The American Western Novel.* New Haven: College and University Press, 1966. Pages 104–13 discuss Wister and *The Virginian,* stressing the insight and skills of the western hero. Excellent overall on the characteristics of the American Western—a good introduction to the genre.

Kemble, Frances Ann. *Journal of a Residence on a Georgian Plantation in 1838–1839.* Edited by John A. Scott. New York: Alfred A. Knopf, 1961. Reprint of the 1863 edition. Fanny Kemble's classic diatribe against the South and slavery. Invaluable for an understanding of her character and Wister's heritage.

Lovering, Joseph P. *S. Weir Mitchell.* Boston: Twayne, 1971. A study of Wister's cousin and literary mentor.

Lukacs, John. *Philadelphia: Patricians and Philistines, 1900–1950.* New York: Farrar Straus Giroux, 1981. Pages 240–57 profile Wister.

Milton, John R. *The Novel of the American West.* Lincoln: University of Nebraska Press, 1980. Weak on Wister, but a thorough presentation of the genre.

Morison, Samuel Eliot. *The Oxford History of the American People.* New York: Oxford, 1965. Pages 521 ff. deal with Wister as the friend and representative of big business against homesteaders in the Johnson County war.

Mott, Frank L. *Golden Multitudes: The Story of Best Sellers in the United States.* New York: Macmillan, 1947. Pages 236–37 deal with the enormous popularity of *The Virginian.*

Webb, Walter Prescott. *The Great Plains.* Boston: Ginn, 1931. Still the best basic background on the cattle kingdom. Invaluable for assessing the context and accuracy of Wister's Western writing.

Ziff, Larzer. *The American 1890s.* New York: Viking, 1966. Pages 224–28 discuss Wister as a writer of the "new strenuousness" that swept America before the turn of the century. Suggests that the Virginian is a forerunner of Hemingway's Nick Adams.

4. Articles

Barsness, John A. "Theodore Roosevelt as Cowboy: The Virginian as Jacksonian Man." *American Quarterly* 21 (Fall 1969):609–19. The best treatment of the "cowboy" aspect of Roosevelt and his relationship with Wister.

Boatright, Mody C. "The American Myth Rides the Range: Owen Wister's Man on Horseback." *Southwest Review* 36 (Summer 1951):157–63. Wister is the first "troubadour" to give the cowboy folk hero a national hearing. *The Virginian* is a chivalric romance and "Horatio Alger story."

Bode, Carl. "Henry James and Owen Wister." *American Literature* 26, no. 2 (May 1954):250–52. Stresses basic dissimilarity of the two men.

Boynton, H. W. "A Word on the 'Genteel Critic.' " *Dial* 59 (14 October 1915):303–6. A discussion of Wister's famous attack on popular literature and the critics who pander to it.

Cobbs, John L. "Charleston: The Image of Aristocracy in Owen Wister's *Lady Baltimore.*" *South Carolina Review* 9 (November 1976):44–51. *Lady Baltimore* is representative of Wister's fiction and reflects social attitudes found in the Western writing.

DeVoto, Bernard. "The Easy Chair: Birth of an Art." *Harper's* 211 (December 1955):8–9 ff. Attacks Wister for "inventing horse opera" instead of dealing realistically with the West. He "created a sun god in leather pants" who has been endlessly imitated ever since.

Heatherington, Madelon E. "Romance without Women: The Sterile Fiction of the American West." *Georgia Review* 33 (1979):643–56. A feminist discussion of Wister, Thomas Berger, and Ken Kesey.

Hough, Robert L., ed. Introduction to *The West of Owen Wister: Selected Short Stories.* Lincoln: University of Nebraska Press, 1972, pp. vii–xvii. A weak and superficial introduction. Unfortunately, this is the only edition of Wister's stories (six) in print.

Hubbell, Jay B. "Owen Wister's Work." *South Atlantic Quarterly* 29 (October 1930):440–43. Reviews Wister's work, discusses the success of *The Virginian,* praises *Lady Baltimore* as an accurate portrait of the South.

Lambert, Neal. "Owen Wister's Lin McLean: The Failure of the Vernacular Hero." *Western American Literature* 5 (Fall 1970):219–32. The most substantial recent treatment of *Lin McLean.*

————. "The Values of the Frontier: Owen Wister's Final Assessment." *South Dakota Review* 9 (Spring 1971):99–107. Sees Wister qualifying his early, idealistic vision of the Saxon cowboy. Very thorough on later fiction, particularly "The Right Honorable the Strawberries."

————. "Owen Wister's Virginian: The Genesis of a Cultural Hero." *Western American Literature* 6 (Summer 1971):99–107. The Virginian is emblematic of a synthesis of eastern and western value systems.

Lewis, Marvin. "Owen Wister: Caste Imprints in Western Letters." *Arizona Quarterly* 10 (Summer 1954):147–56. "Wister created in fiction the triumph of the authoritarians over the rough libertarians of the West." A thoughtful assessment of Wister's antiegalitarianism.

Lukacs, John. "From Camelot to Abilene." *American Heritage* 32 (February-March 1981):52–57. Accents Wister's melancholia and the incongruity of an aristocrat dealing with the crude frontier.

Marovitz, Sanford E. "Testament of a Patriot: The Virginian, the Tenderfoot, and Owen Wister." *Texas Studies in Literature and Language* 15 (Fall 1973):551–75. Discusses the Virginian and the narrator of the novel as representatives of their respective regions.

Mason, Julian. "Owen Wister and the South." *Southern Humanities Review* 6 (Winter 1972):23–34. Wister's southern heritage and lifelong affinity for the South.

————. "Owen Wister and World War I: Appeal for Pentecost." *Pennsylvania Magazine of History and Biography* 101 (1977):89–102. One of the few studies of Wister's World War I trilogy.

Percy, Walker. "Decline of the Western." *Commonweal* 68 (16 May 1958):181–83. Says *The Virginian* is still "the best western," and traces its chivalric roots.

Robinson, Forrest G. "The Roosevelt-Wister Connection." *Western American Literature* 14 (1979):95–114. Title self-explanatory.

Seelye, John. "When West Was Wister." *New Republic* 167 (2 September 1972):28–33. An extensive review of Ben Merchant Vorpahl's *My Dear Wister,* with commentary on Wister and the projection of the mythic West.

Solensten, John M. "Richard Harding Davis, Owen Wister, and the Virginian: Unpublished Letters and a Commentary." *American Literary Realism: 1870–1910* 5 (Spring 1972):122–33. Letters from Wister to Davis delineating his conception of the Virginian as an emblematic American hero.

Stegner, Wallace. "Owen Wister: Creator of the Cowboy Myth": *American West* 21, no. 1 (January/February 1984), pp. 48–52. Profile of Wister accompanying first publication of "Chalkeye," from a recently discovered manuscript of what may be Wister's first Western story.

Vorpahl, Ben Merchant. "Ernest Hemingway and Owen Wister." *Library Chronicle* 36 (Spring 1970):126–37. A largely historical study of the relationship between the two men. Scholarly and well-written, it traces a potential influence on Hemingway that is too often ignored by critics.

————. "Henry James and Owen Wister." *Pennsylvania Magazine of History and Biography* 95 (July 1971):291–338. A thorough and well-written explication of Wister and James and the enormous impact of the latter on Wister's writing and literary philosophy. An important article.

————. "Very Much Like a Fire-cracker: Owen Wister on Mark Twain." *Western American Literature* 6 (Summer 1971):83–98. Discusses Wister's 1935 *Harper's* essay, "In Homage to Mark Twain," accenting Wister's defense of Twain's lack of formal education and his fascination with Twain's bitterness near the end of his life. Also, perceptive comparison of Wister and Howells.

Walker, Don D. "Wister, Roosevelt and James: A Note on the Western." *American Quarterly* 12 (Fall 1960):358–66. Claims Wister avoided unpleasant reality and was deterred from portraying it by objections of Roosevelt and James.

Williams, John. "The Western: Definition of the Myth." *Nation* 193 (18 November 1961):402 ff. Perceptive on the philosophical roots of the characterization of the Virginian—an Emersonian and a Calvinist.

Woollcott, Alexander. "Wisteria." *New Yorker* 6 (30 August 1930):30. A savage attack on Wister's snobbishness, branding his biography of Roosevelt "aristocratic" and calling Wister "a deep-dyed product of feudal Philadelphia."

5. Dissertations

Lambert, Neal. "The Western Writings of Owen Wister: The Conflict of East and West." University of Utah, 1966 (DA: 27, 2503A). Sees Wister as dealing with the problems of eastern "civilization" versus western freedom and lack of order. At first Wister saw "vernacular goodness" in the West, but disillusionment led to qualification of this vision. See Lambert's article, "The Values of the Frontier: Owen Wister's Final Assessment."

Watkins, George Thomas. "Owen Wister and the American West: A Biographical and Critical Study." University of Illinois, 1959 (DA: 20, 1172). The best and most complete full-length work on Wister. Excellent as a literary biography tracing Wister's life and work. Particularly strong on biographical material.

Witkowsky, Paul William. "The Idea of Order: Frontier Societies in the Fiction of Cooper, Simms, Hawthorne, and Wister." University of North Carolina at Chapel Hill, 1979 (DAI: 40, 3306A). Unsympathetic treatment of Wister's authoritarianism and racism, but excellent tracing the roots of Wister's thought to nineteenth-century philosophies, particularly social Darwinism.

6. Other Sources

Folsom, James K. *The Works of Owen Wister*. Deland, Fla.: Everett-Edwards, Inc., 1978. Taped lecture: Western American Writers Series, no. 1121.

Index

DATE DUE
